Walt Disney's Comics

THUG BUSTERS *starring Donald Duck*
Story & Art: Carl Barks *(WDC 61, October 1945)* • **Color:** Susan Daigle-Leach

MICKEY'S DANGEROUS DOUBLE Part Two *starring Mickey Mouse*
Story: Bill Walsh • **Art:** Floyd Gottfredson *(KFS 3/7-6/22/53)* • **Color:** Disney Italia

FOR SCHOOL THE BELL TOLLS *starring Donald Duck*
Story: Paul Halas & Unn Printz-Påhlson • **Art:** Vicar
Color: Egmont & David Gerstein • **Dialogue & Lettering:** David Gerstein

SIMIAN SIMILARITY *starring Fethry Duck*
Story: Stefan Petrucha • **Art:** Tino Santanach
Color: Egmont • **Lettering:** David Gerstein

BRER RABBIT'S SECRET *starring Brer Rabbit*
Story: Unknown • **Art:** Paul Murry *(Cheerios Giveaway Y2, 1947)*
Color: Sanoma & David Gerstein

THE PHONEY *starring Donald Duck*
Story & Art: William Van Horn • **Color:** Egmont

Front cover art by Carl Barks, color by Susan Daigle-Leach

A Look At Next Month

Walt Disney's Comics and Stories 685: It's time for Halloween! Fan favorite Marco Rota strands Donald and Daisy at "The Hada House," a mansion owned by a very rich vampire! Next, Romano Scarpa confronts Mickey with shape-shifting "Transmutant Gifts"; then Carl Barks transforms Donald into a "Jet Witch"! Finally we shift gears to celebrate Huey, Dewey and Louie's 70th anniversary with Pat and Carol McGreal's "Happy Birthday... Times Three"!

Uncle Scrooge 370: When Scrooge swaps places with Giorgio Cavazzano's "Brother From Another Earth," he winds up in a scary parallel Duckburg! Magica sics a ghost on Scrooge in Frank Jonker's "Spirit of Fear"; then Scrooge battles a giant robot in Lars Jensen's "Synthezoid from the Deepest Void!" Finally, in Carl Barks' "That Small Feeling," Gyro Gearloose meets the witch doctor—and gets his head shrunk before you can say ooh-ee-ooh-ah-ah!

www.gemstonepub.com/disney

STEPHEN A. GEPPI - President/Publisher and Chief Executive Officer • JOHN K. SNYDER JR. - Chief Administrative Officer
STAFF: LEONARD (JOHN) CLARK - Editor-in-Chief • SUE KOLBERG - Assistant Editor
TRAVIS SEITLER - Art Director • DAVID GERSTEIN - Archival Editor
CONTRIBUTING STAFF: GARY LEACH & SUSAN DAIGLE-LEACH - Art & Editorial
ADVERTISING/MARKETING: J.C. VAUGHN - Executive Editor/Associate Publisher • BRENDA BUSICK - Creative Director
HEATHER WINTER - Office Manager Toll Free (888) 375-9800 Ext. 249
MARK HUESMAN - Production Assistant • MIKE WILBUR - Shipping Manager • RALPH TURNER - Accounting Manager
ANGIE MEYER & JUDY GOODWIN - Subscriptions Toll Free (800) 322-7978

Walt Disney's Comics and Stories No. 684, September 2007. Published monthly by Gemstone Publishing. © 2007 Disney Enterprises, Inc., except where noted. All rights reserved. Nothing contained herein may be reproduced without the written permission of Disney Enterprises, Inc., Burbank, CA, or other copyright holders. 12-issue subscription rates: In the U.S., $83.40. In Canada, $90.00, payable in U.S. funds. For advertising rates and information call (888) 375-9800 ext. 410. Subscription and advertising rates subject to change without notice. Postmaster: send address changes to Walt Disney's Comics & Stories, PO Box 469, West Plains, MO 65775. PRINTED IN CANADA

Walt Disney presents
DONALD DUCK

HAND ME THE MICROSCOPE PLEASE, INSPECTOR HUEY!

RIGHTO, INSPECTOR DEWEY!

INSPECTOR LOUIE, WHILE I EXAMINE THIS HAIR FROM THE HEAD OF THE VICTIM, WILL YOU AND INSPECTOR HUEY LOOK UP THE VICTIM'S LAUNDRY MARKS?

THE KIDS ARE PLAYING THEY'RE DETECTIVES!

THUG BUSTERS INC.

I'LL GIVE A REPORT ON THIS HAIR AS SOON AS I GET THE MICROSCOPE FOCUSED!

COME TO PAPA, LITTLE CENTIPEDE! THIS OPPORTUNITY IS TOO SWEET TO MISS!

ONE MORE TURN OF THE KNOB AND THIS HAIR WILL BE MAGNIFIED A THOUSAND TIMES!

EEK!

WHAT COULD HAVE UPSET INSPECTOR DEWEY?

HE FAINTED DEAD AWAY!

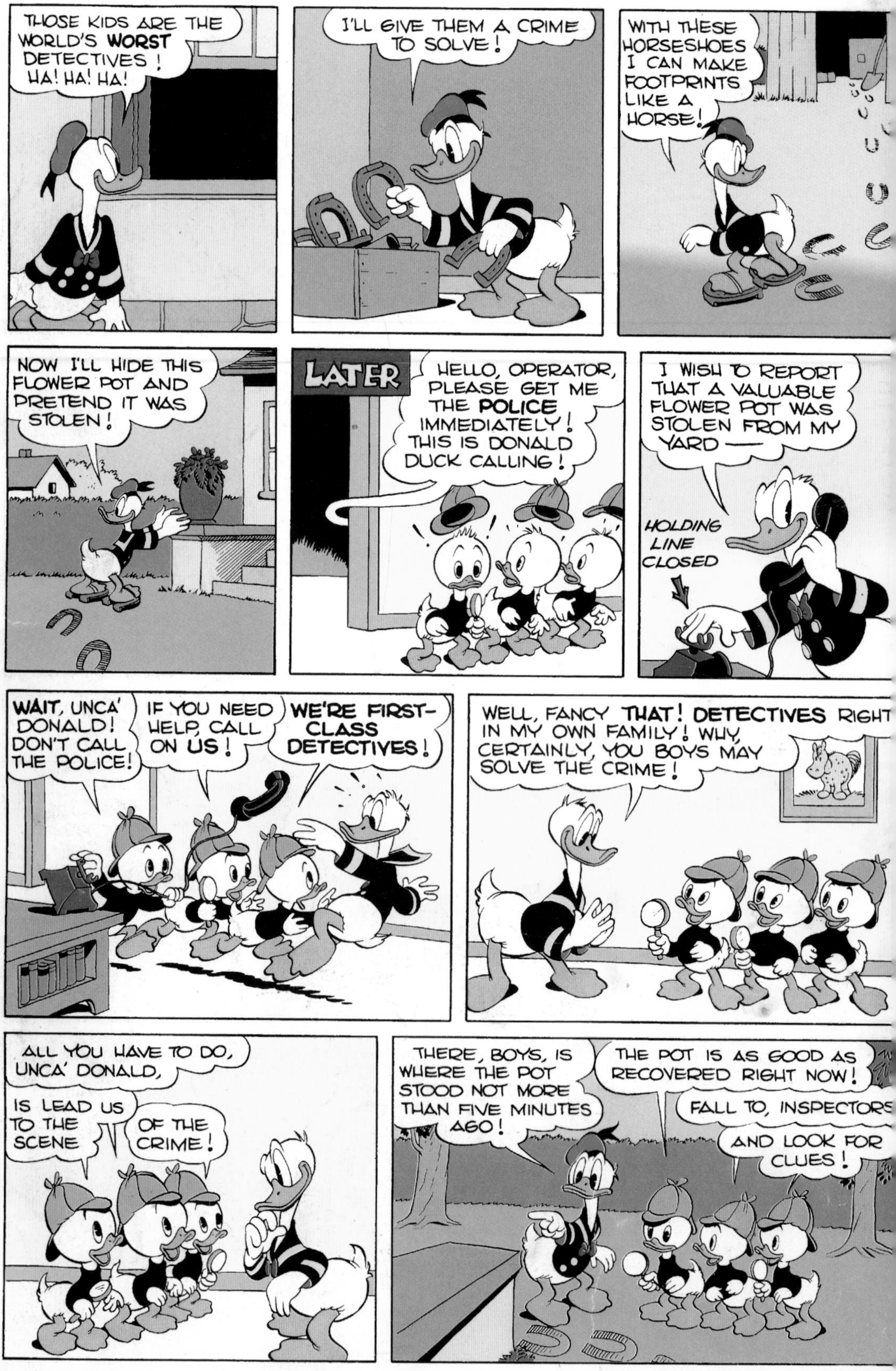

THOSE KIDS ARE THE WORLD'S **WORST** DETECTIVES! HA! HA! HA!
I'LL GIVE THEM A CRIME TO SOLVE!
WITH THESE HORSESHOES I CAN MAKE FOOTPRINTS LIKE A HORSE!
NOW I'LL HIDE THIS FLOWER POT AND PRETEND IT WAS STOLEN!
LATER
HELLO, OPERATOR, PLEASE GET ME THE **POLICE** IMMEDIATELY! THIS IS DONALD DUCK CALLING!
I WISH TO REPORT THAT A VALUABLE FLOWER POT WAS STOLEN FROM MY YARD —
HOLDING LINE CLOSED
WAIT, UNCA' DONALD! DON'T CALL THE POLICE!
IF YOU NEED HELP, CALL ON **US**!
WE'RE FIRST-CLASS DETECTIVES!
WELL, FANCY **THAT**! **DETECTIVES** RIGHT IN MY OWN FAMILY! WHY, CERTAINLY, YOU BOYS MAY SOLVE THE CRIME!
ALL YOU HAVE TO DO, UNCA' DONALD,
IS LEAD US TO THE SCENE
OF THE CRIME!
THERE, BOYS, IS WHERE THE POT STOOD NOT MORE THAN FIVE MINUTES AGO!
THE POT IS AS GOOD AS RECOVERED RIGHT NOW!
FALL TO, INSPECTORS
AND LOOK FOR CLUES!

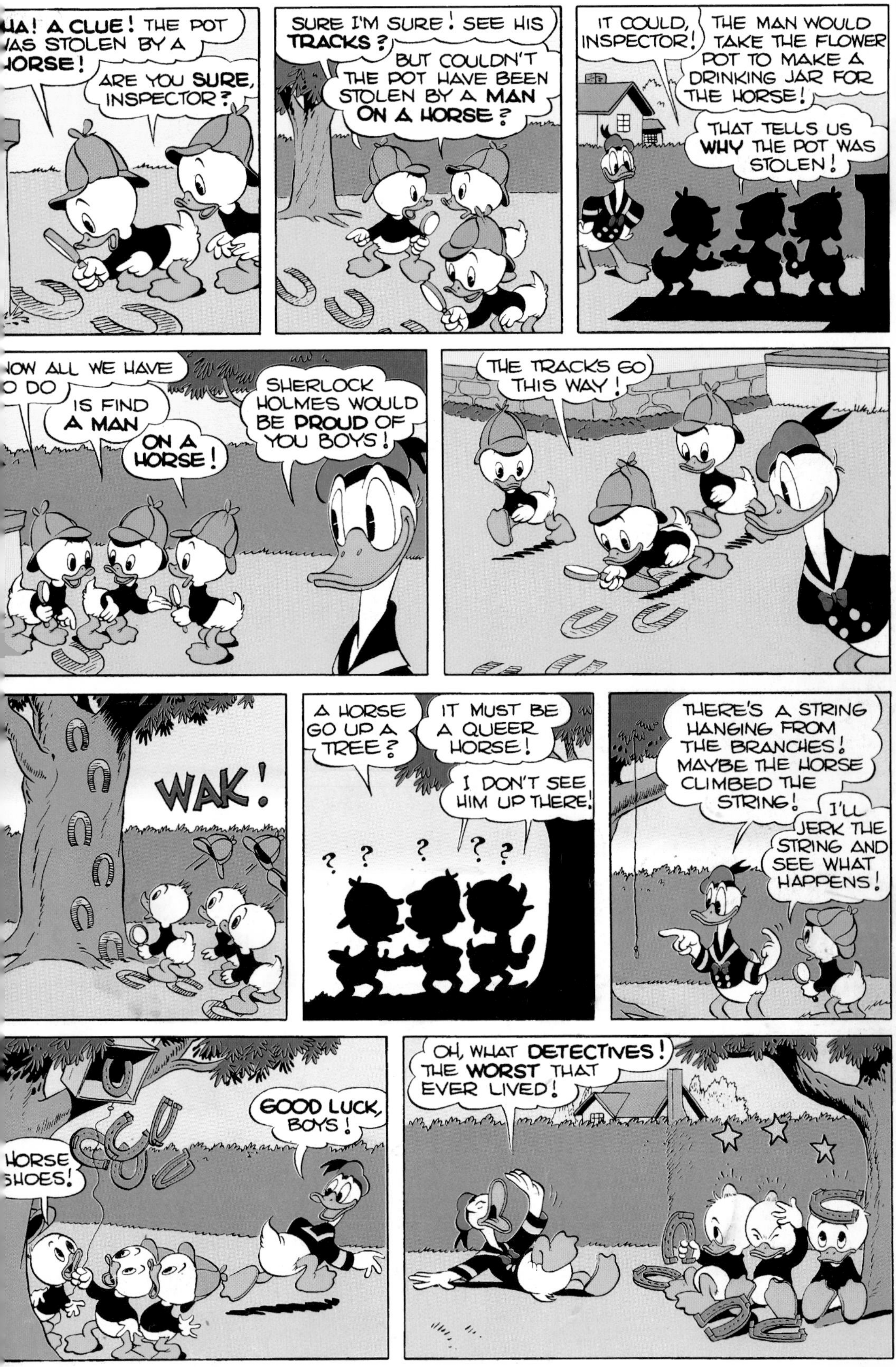
HA! A CLUE! THE POT WAS STOLEN BY A HORSE!
ARE YOU SURE, INSPECTOR?
SURE I'M SURE! SEE HIS TRACKS?
BUT COULDN'T THE POT HAVE BEEN STOLEN BY A MAN ON A HORSE?
IT COULD, INSPECTOR!
THE MAN WOULD TAKE THE FLOWER POT TO MAKE A DRINKING JAR FOR THE HORSE!
THAT TELLS US WHY THE POT WAS STOLEN!
NOW ALL WE HAVE TO DO
IS FIND A MAN
ON A HORSE!
SHERLOCK HOLMES WOULD BE PROUD OF YOU BOYS!
THE TRACKS GO THIS WAY!
WAK!
A HORSE GO UP A TREE?
IT MUST BE A QUEER HORSE!
I DON'T SEE HIM UP THERE!
? ? ? ? ?
THERE'S A STRING HANGING FROM THE BRANCHES! MAYBE THE HORSE CLIMBED THE STRING!
I'LL JERK THE STRING AND SEE WHAT HAPPENS!
HORSE SHOES!
GOOD LUCK, BOYS!
OH, WHAT DETECTIVES! THE WORST THAT EVER LIVED!

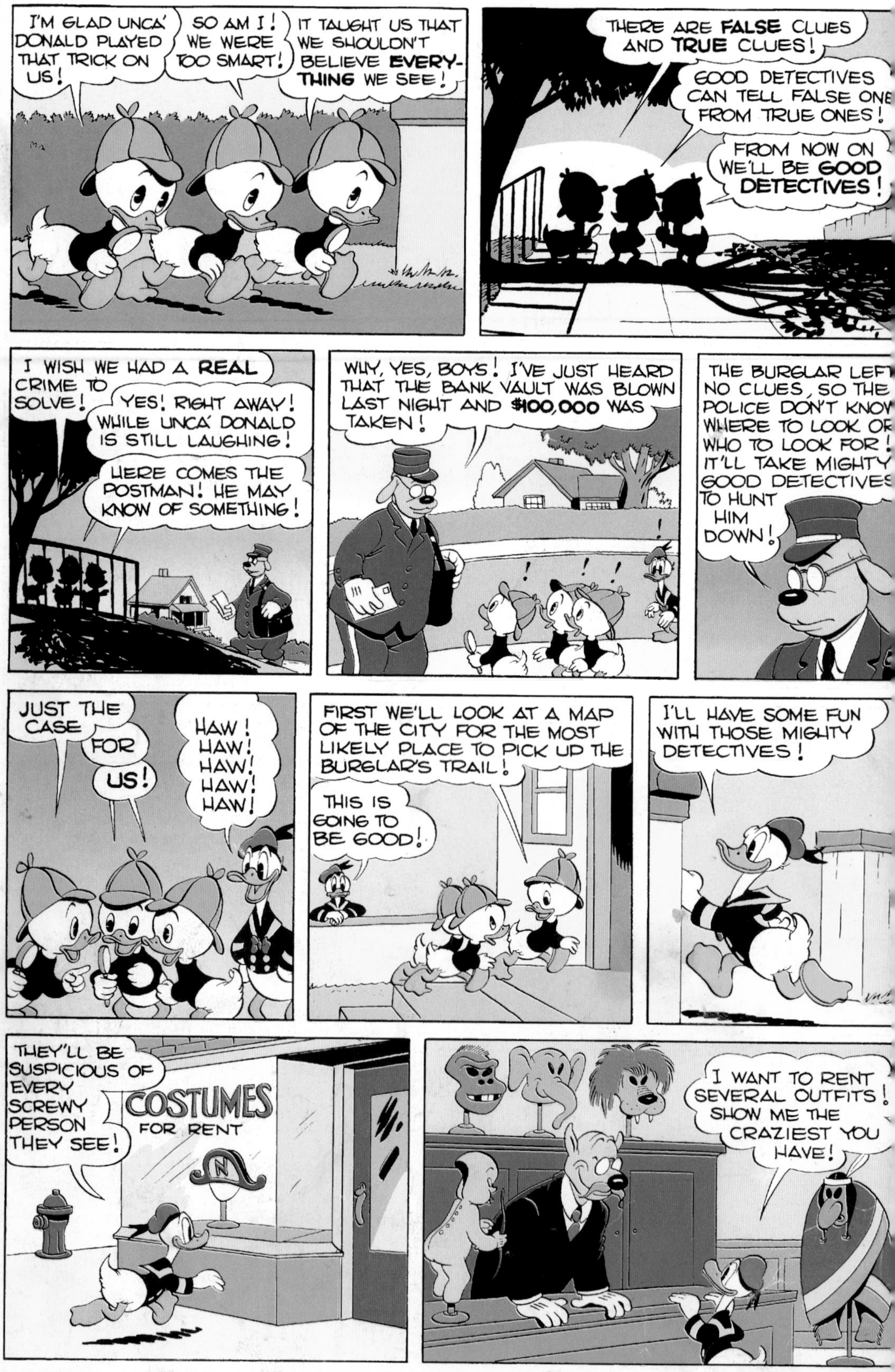

I'M GLAD UNCA' DONALD PLAYED THAT TRICK ON US!
SO AM I! WE WERE TOO SMART!
IT TAUGHT US THAT WE SHOULDN'T BELIEVE EVERYTHING WE SEE!
THERE ARE FALSE CLUES AND TRUE CLUES!
GOOD DETECTIVES CAN TELL FALSE ONE FROM TRUE ONES!
FROM NOW ON WE'LL BE GOOD DETECTIVES!
I WISH WE HAD A REAL CRIME TO SOLVE!
YES! RIGHT AWAY! WHILE UNCA' DONALD IS STILL LAUGHING!
HERE COMES THE POSTMAN! HE MAY KNOW OF SOMETHING!
WHY, YES, BOYS! I'VE JUST HEARD THAT THE BANK VAULT WAS BLOWN LAST NIGHT AND $100,000 WAS TAKEN!
THE BURGLAR LEFT NO CLUES, SO THE POLICE DON'T KNOW WHERE TO LOOK OR WHO TO LOOK FOR! IT'LL TAKE MIGHTY GOOD DETECTIVES TO HUNT HIM DOWN!
JUST THE CASE
FOR
US!
HAW! HAW! HAW! HAW! HAW!
FIRST WE'LL LOOK AT A MAP OF THE CITY FOR THE MOST LIKELY PLACE TO PICK UP THE BURGLAR'S TRAIL!
THIS IS GOING TO BE GOOD!
I'LL HAVE SOME FUN WITH THOSE MIGHTY DETECTIVES!
THEY'LL BE SUSPICIOUS OF EVERY SCREWY PERSON THEY SEE!
COSTUMES FOR RENT
I WANT TO RENT SEVERAL OUTFITS! SHOW ME THE CRAZIEST YOU HAVE!

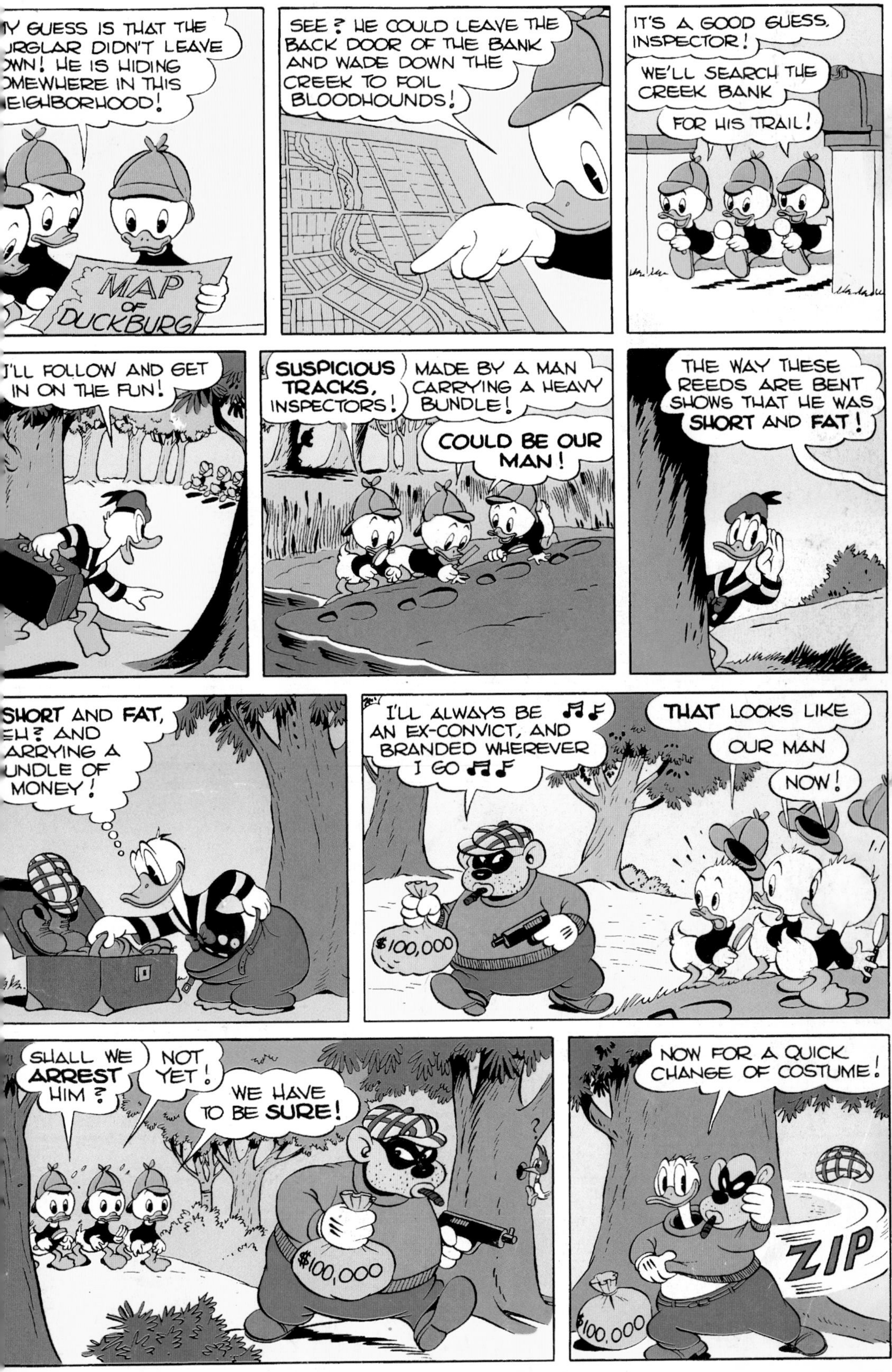

Y GUESS IS THAT THE URGLAR DIDN'T LEAVE OWN! HE IS HIDING OMEWHERE IN THIS EIGHBORHOOD!
MAP OF DUCKBURG
SEE? HE COULD LEAVE THE BACK DOOR OF THE BANK AND WADE DOWN THE CREEK TO FOIL BLOODHOUNDS!
IT'S A GOOD GUESS, INSPECTOR!
WE'LL SEARCH THE CREEK BANK
FOR HIS TRAIL!
I'LL FOLLOW AND GET IN ON THE FUN!
SUSPICIOUS TRACKS, INSPECTORS!
MADE BY A MAN CARRYING A HEAVY BUNDLE!
COULD BE OUR MAN!
THE WAY THESE REEDS ARE BENT SHOWS THAT HE WAS SHORT AND FAT!
SHORT AND FAT, EH? AND ARRYING A UNDLE OF MONEY!
I'LL ALWAYS BE AN EX-CONVICT, AND BRANDED WHEREVER I GO
THAT LOOKS LIKE
OUR MAN
NOW!
$100,000
SHALL WE ARREST HIM?
NOT YET!
WE HAVE TO BE SURE!
$100,000
NOW FOR A QUICK CHANGE OF COSTUME!
ZIP
$100,000

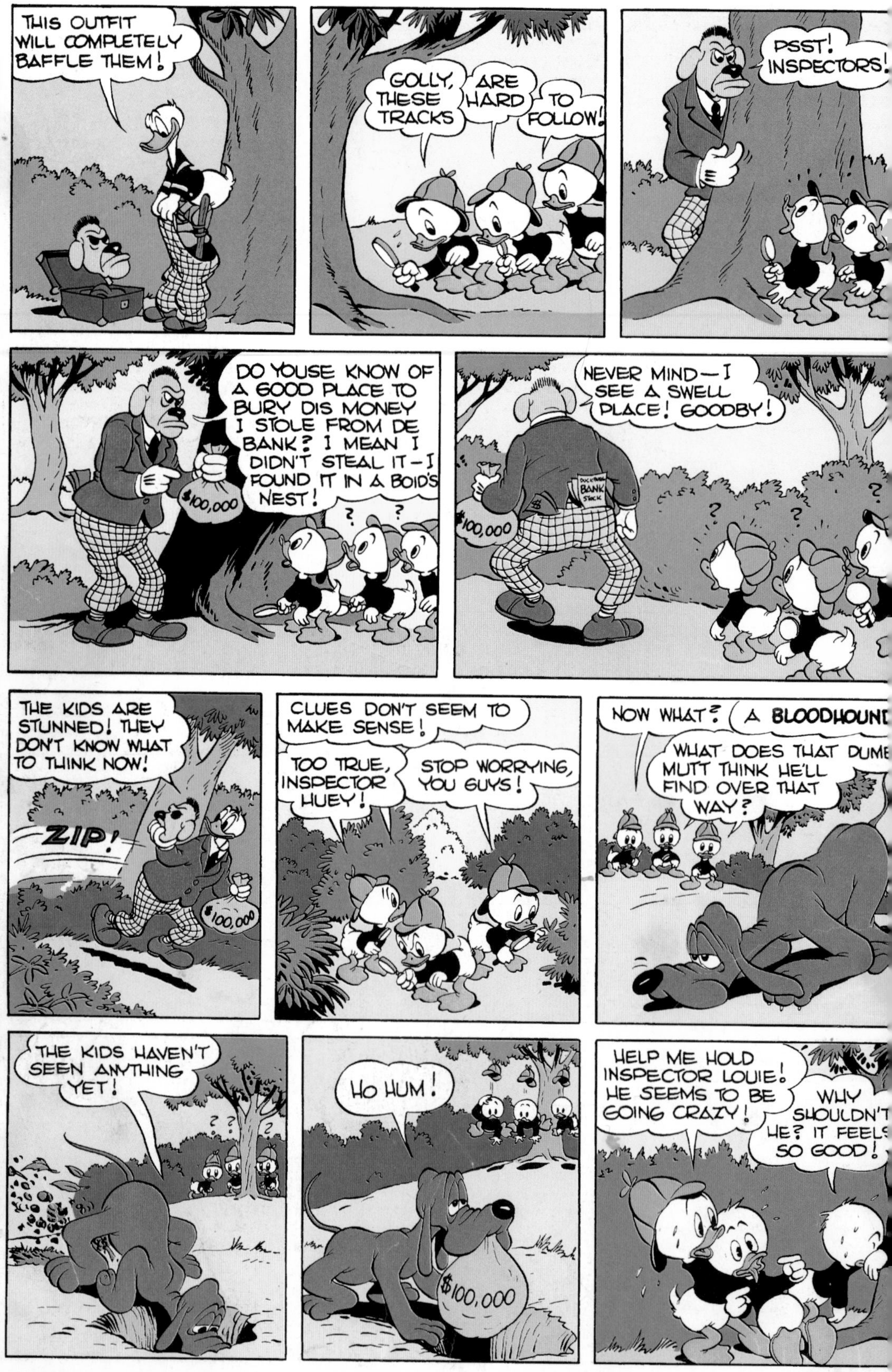
THIS OUTFIT WILL COMPLETELY BAFFLE THEM!
GOLLY, THESE TRACKS
ARE HARD
TO FOLLOW!
PSST! INSPECTORS!
DO YOUSE KNOW OF A GOOD PLACE TO BURY DIS MONEY I STOLE FROM DE BANK? I MEAN I DIDN'T STEAL IT—I FOUND IT IN A BOID'S NEST!
$100,000
NEVER MIND—I SEE A SWELL PLACE! GOODBY!
BANK
$100,000
THE KIDS ARE STUNNED! THEY DON'T KNOW WHAT TO THINK NOW!
ZIP!
$100,000
CLUES DON'T SEEM TO MAKE SENSE!
TOO TRUE, INSPECTOR HUEY!
STOP WORRYING, YOU GUYS!
NOW WHAT?
A BLOODHOUND
WHAT DOES THAT DUMB MUTT THINK HE'LL FIND OVER THAT WAY?
THE KIDS HAVEN'T SEEN ANYTHING YET!
HO HUM!
$100,000
HELP ME HOLD INSPECTOR LOUIE! HE SEEMS TO BE GOING CRAZY!
WHY SHOULDN'T HE? IT FEELS SO GOOD!

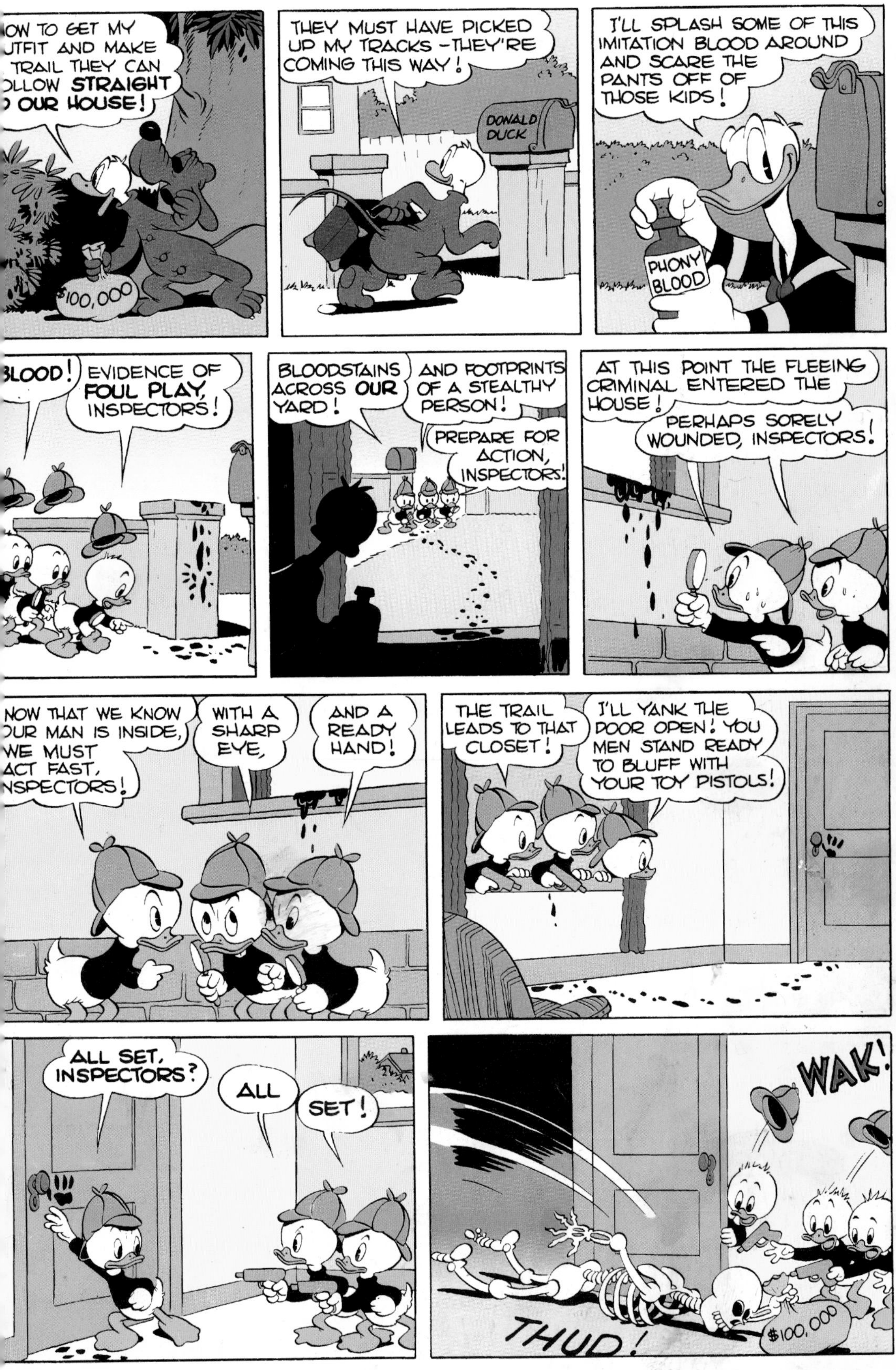

OW TO GET MY
UTFIT AND MAKE
TRAIL THEY CAN
OLLOW STRAIGHT
O OUR HOUSE!
$100,000
THEY MUST HAVE PICKED UP MY TRACKS -THEY'RE COMING THIS WAY!
DONALD DUCK
I'LL SPLASH SOME OF THIS IMITATION BLOOD AROUND AND SCARE THE PANTS OFF OF THOSE KIDS!
PHONY BLOOD
BLOOD!
EVIDENCE OF FOUL PLAY, INSPECTORS!
BLOODSTAINS ACROSS OUR YARD!
AND FOOTPRINTS OF A STEALTHY PERSON!
PREPARE FOR ACTION, INSPECTORS!
AT THIS POINT THE FLEEING CRIMINAL ENTERED THE HOUSE!
PERHAPS SORELY WOUNDED, INSPECTORS!
NOW THAT WE KNOW
OUR MAN IS INSIDE,
WE MUST
ACT FAST,
NSPECTORS!
WITH A SHARP EYE,
AND A READY HAND!
THE TRAIL LEADS TO THAT CLOSET!
I'LL YANK THE DOOR OPEN! YOU MEN STAND READY TO BLUFF WITH YOUR TOY PISTOLS!
ALL SET, INSPECTORS?
ALL
SET!
WAK!
THUD!
$100,000

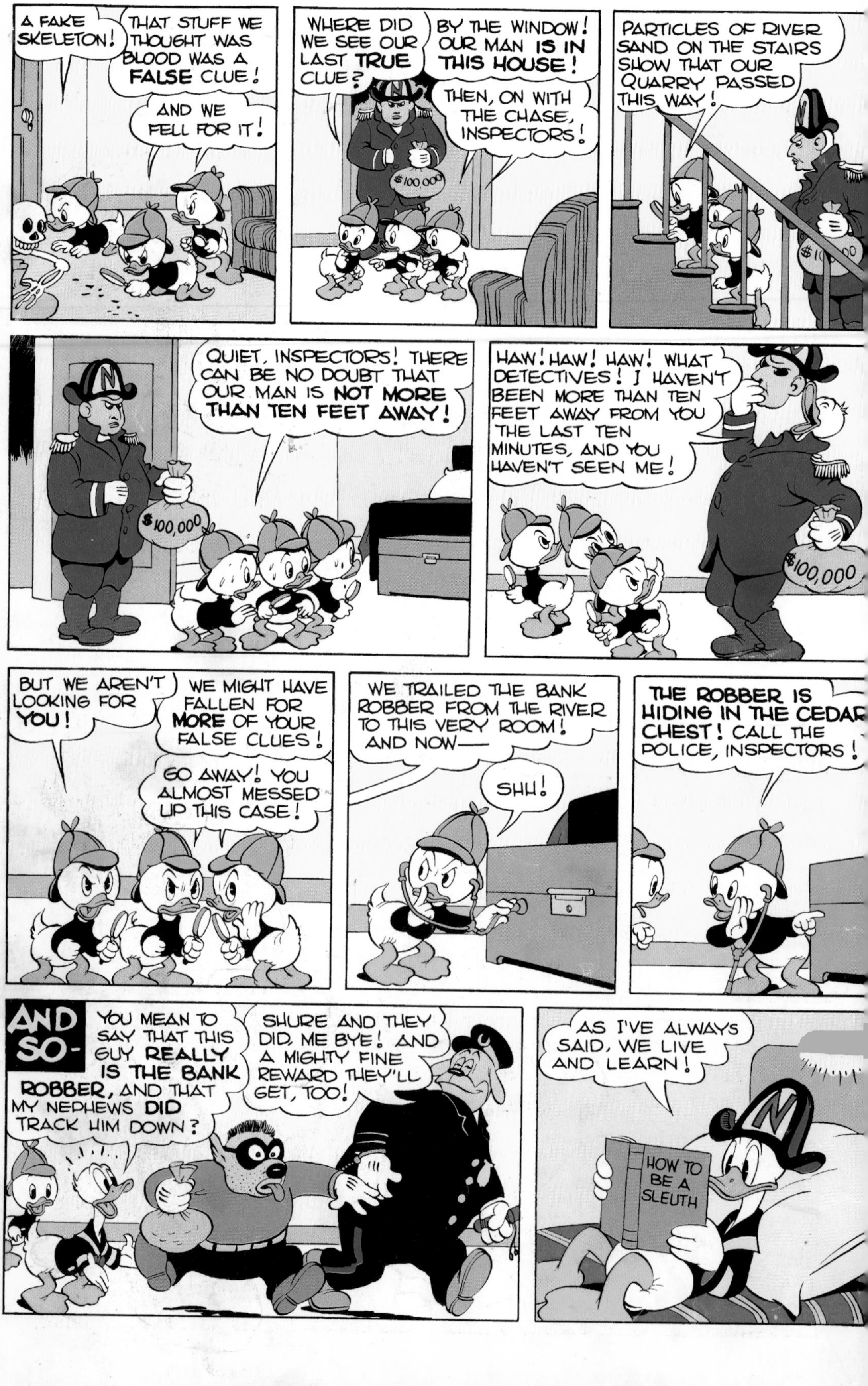

A FAKE SKELETON!
THAT STUFF WE THOUGHT WAS BLOOD WAS A FALSE CLUE!
AND WE FELL FOR IT!
WHERE DID WE SEE OUR LAST TRUE CLUE?
BY THE WINDOW! OUR MAN IS IN THIS HOUSE!
THEN, ON WITH THE CHASE, INSPECTORS!
$100,000
PARTICLES OF RIVER SAND ON THE STAIRS SHOW THAT OUR QUARRY PASSED THIS WAY!
QUIET, INSPECTORS! THERE CAN BE NO DOUBT THAT OUR MAN IS NOT MORE THAN TEN FEET AWAY!
$100,000
HAW! HAW! HAW! WHAT DETECTIVES! I HAVEN'T BEEN MORE THAN TEN FEET AWAY FROM YOU THE LAST TEN MINUTES, AND YOU HAVEN'T SEEN ME!
$100,000
BUT WE AREN'T LOOKING FOR YOU!
WE MIGHT HAVE FALLEN FOR MORE OF YOUR FALSE CLUES!
GO AWAY! YOU ALMOST MESSED UP THIS CASE!
WE TRAILED THE BANK ROBBER FROM THE RIVER TO THIS VERY ROOM! AND NOW—
SHH!
THE ROBBER IS HIDING IN THE CEDAR CHEST! CALL THE POLICE, INSPECTORS!
AND SO-
YOU MEAN TO SAY THAT THIS GUY REALLY IS THE BANK ROBBER, AND THAT MY NEPHEWS DID TRACK HIM DOWN?
SHURE AND THEY DID, ME BYE! AND A MIGHTY FINE REWARD THEY'LL GET, TOO!
AS I'VE ALWAYS SAID, WE LIVE AND LEARN!
HOW TO BE A SLEUTH

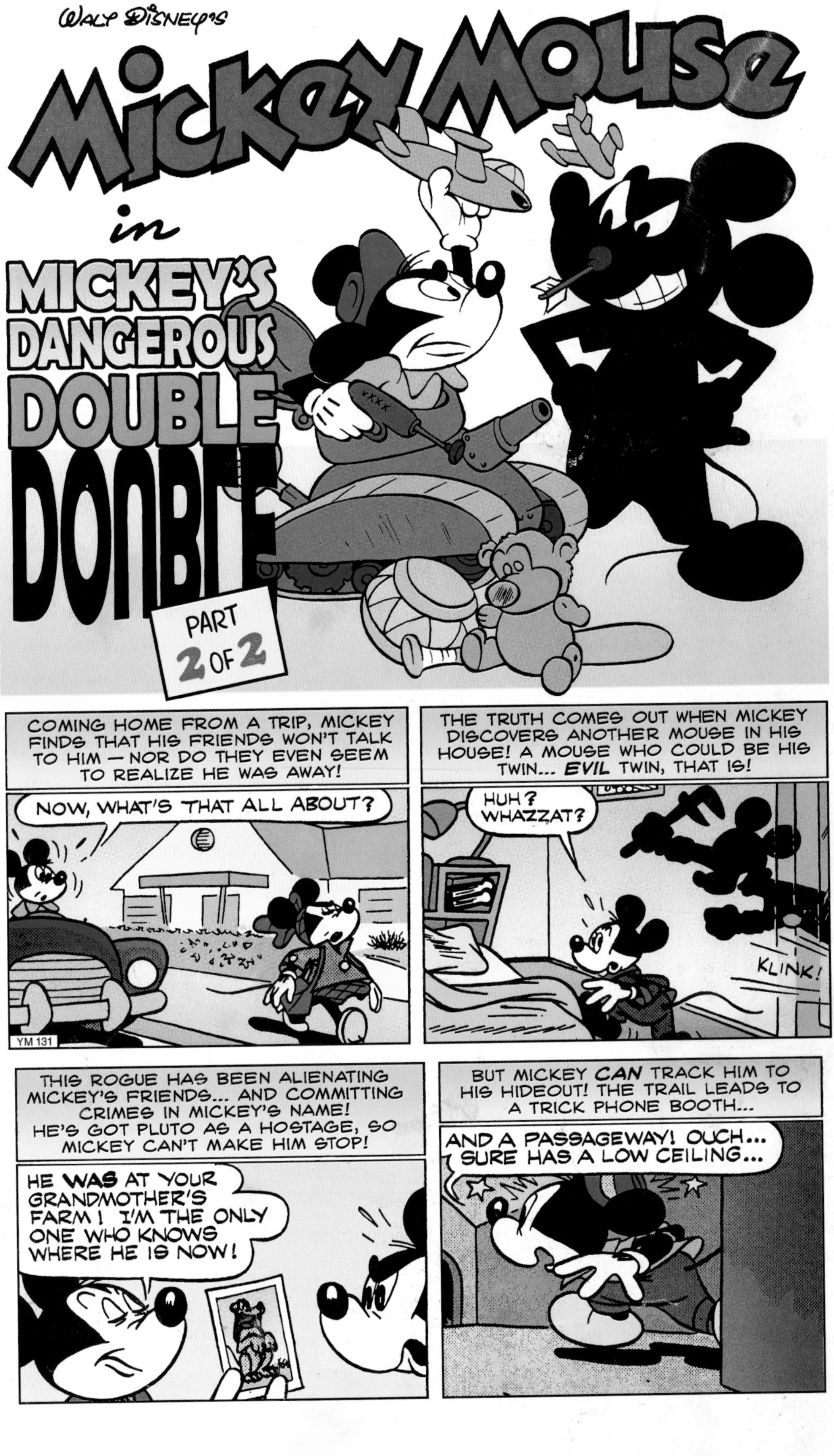

WALT DISNEY'S
MICKEY MOUSE
in
MICKEY'S DANGEROUS DOUBLE
PART 2 OF 2
COMING HOME FROM A TRIP, MICKEY FINDS THAT HIS FRIENDS WON'T TALK TO HIM — NOR DO THEY EVEN SEEM TO REALIZE HE WAS AWAY!
NOW, WHAT'S THAT ALL ABOUT?
YM 131
THE TRUTH COMES OUT WHEN MICKEY DISCOVERS ANOTHER MOUSE IN HIS HOUSE! A MOUSE WHO COULD BE HIS TWIN... EVIL TWIN, THAT IS!
HUH? WHAZZAT?
KLINK!
THIS ROGUE HAS BEEN ALIENATING MICKEY'S FRIENDS... AND COMMITTING CRIMES IN MICKEY'S NAME! HE'S GOT PLUTO AS A HOSTAGE, SO MICKEY CAN'T MAKE HIM STOP!
HE WAS AT YOUR GRANDMOTHER'S FARM! I'M THE ONLY ONE WHO KNOWS WHERE HE IS NOW!
BUT MICKEY CAN TRACK HIM TO HIS HIDEOUT! THE TRAIL LEADS TO A TRICK PHONE BOOTH...
AND A PASSAGEWAY! OUCH... SURE HAS A LOW CEILING...

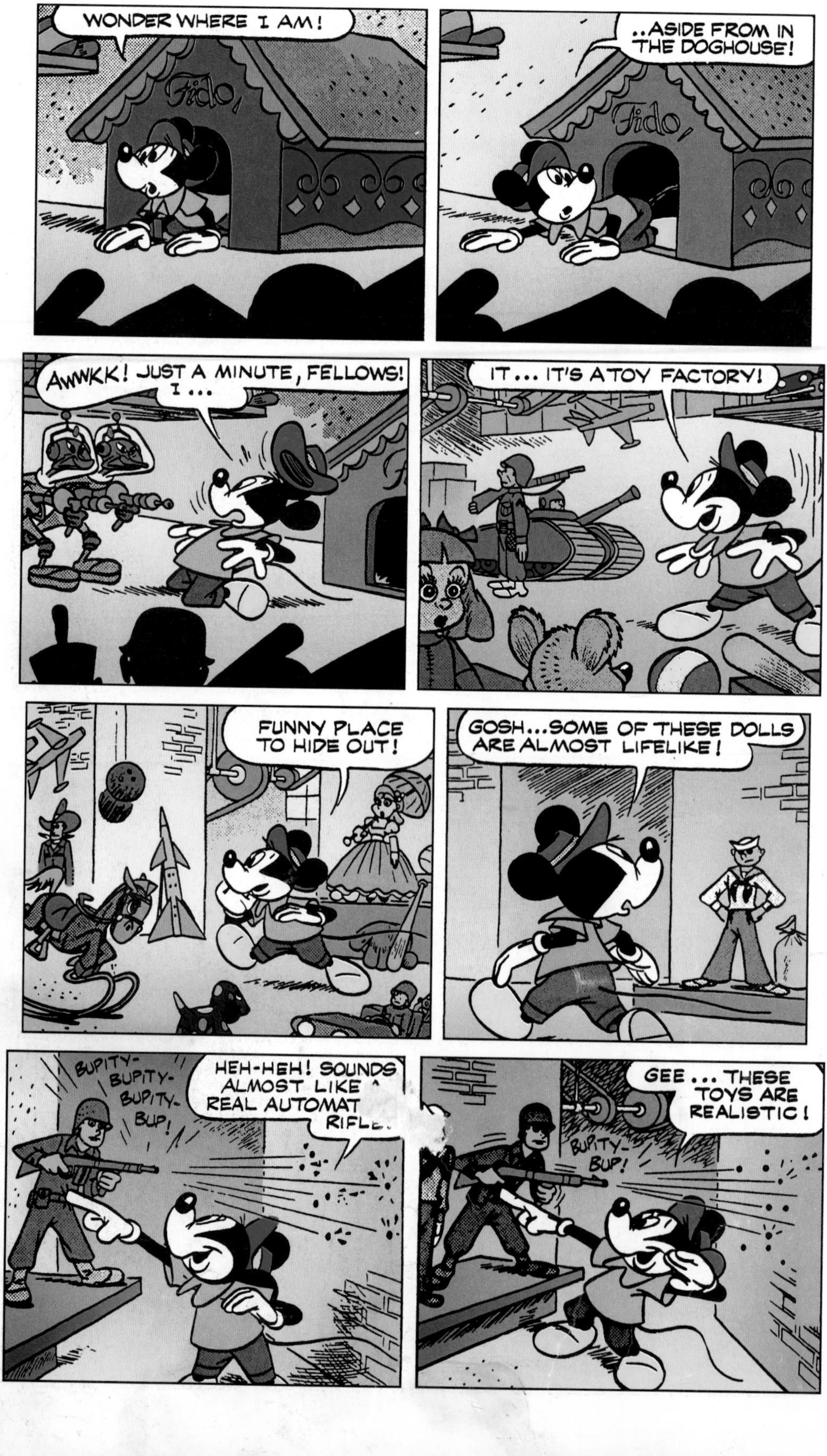
WONDER WHERE I AM!
Fido
..ASIDE FROM IN THE DOGHOUSE!
Fido
AWWKK! JUST A MINUTE, FELLOWS! I...
IT... IT'S A TOY FACTORY!
FUNNY PLACE TO HIDE OUT!
GOSH...SOME OF THESE DOLLS ARE ALMOST LIFELIKE!
BUPITY-BUPITY-BUPITY-BUP!
HEH-HEH! SOUNDS ALMOST LIKE A REAL AUTOMAT RIFLE
BUPITY-BUP!
GEE... THESE TOYS ARE REALISTIC!

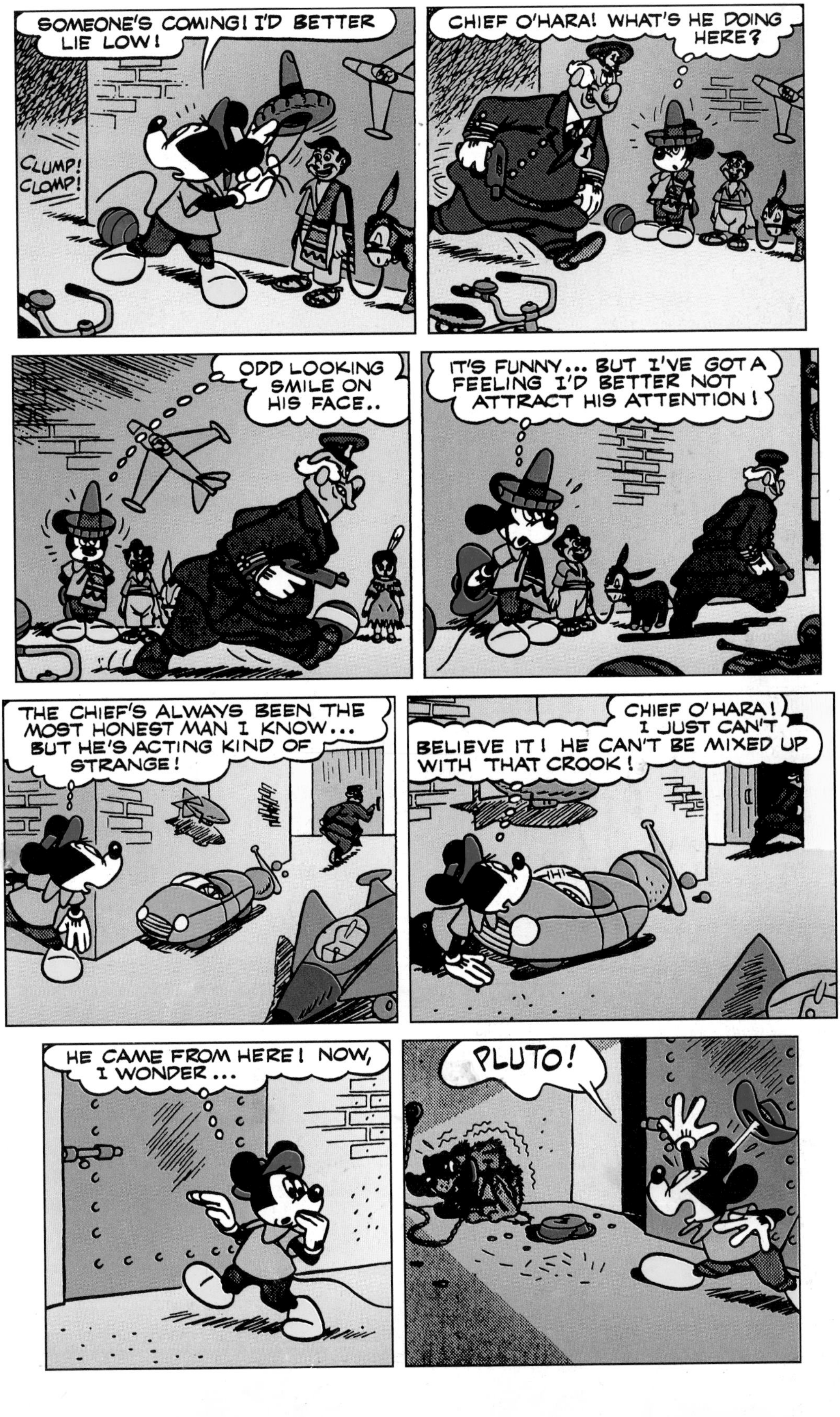
SOMEONE'S COMING! I'D BETTER LIE LOW!
CLUMP! CLOMP!
CHIEF O'HARA! WHAT'S HE DOING HERE?
ODD LOOKING SMILE ON HIS FACE..
IT'S FUNNY... BUT I'VE GOT A FEELING I'D BETTER NOT ATTRACT HIS ATTENTION!
THE CHIEF'S ALWAYS BEEN THE MOST HONEST MAN I KNOW... BUT HE'S ACTING KIND OF STRANGE!
CHIEF O'HARA! I JUST CAN'T BELIEVE IT! HE CAN'T BE MIXED UP WITH THAT CROOK!
HE CAME FROM HERE! NOW, I WONDER...
PLUTO!

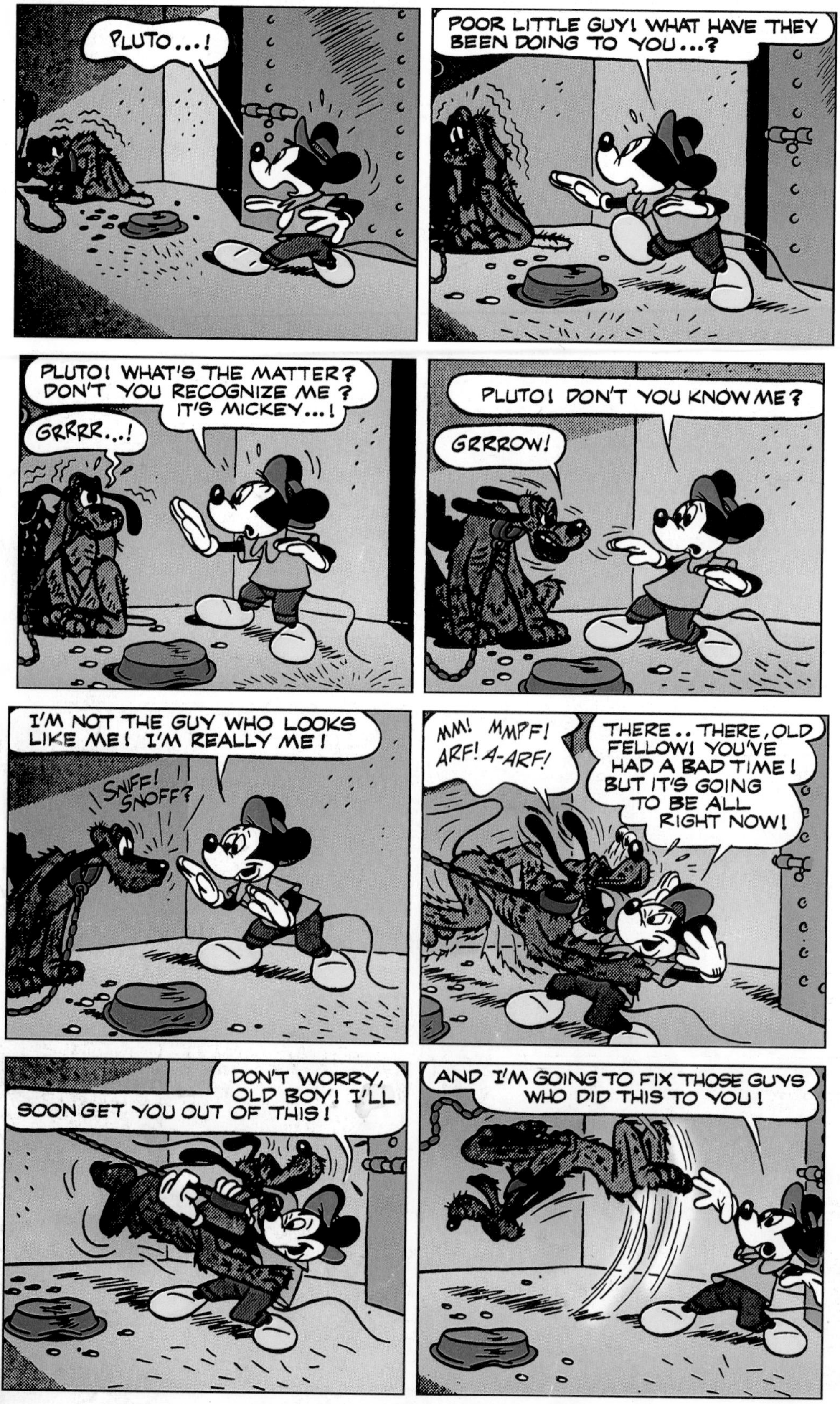
PLUTO...!
POOR LITTLE GUY! WHAT HAVE THEY BEEN DOING TO YOU...?
PLUTO! WHAT'S THE MATTER? DON'T YOU RECOGNIZE ME? IT'S MICKEY...!
GRRRR...!
PLUTO! DON'T YOU KNOW ME?
GRRROW!
I'M NOT THE GUY WHO LOOKS LIKE ME! I'M REALLY ME!
SNIFF! SNOFF?
MM! MMPF! ARF! A-ARF!
THERE.. THERE, OLD FELLOW! YOU'VE HAD A BAD TIME! BUT IT'S GOING TO BE ALL RIGHT NOW!
DON'T WORRY, OLD BOY! I'LL SOON GET YOU OUT OF THIS!
AND I'M GOING TO FIX THOSE GUYS WHO DID THIS TO YOU!

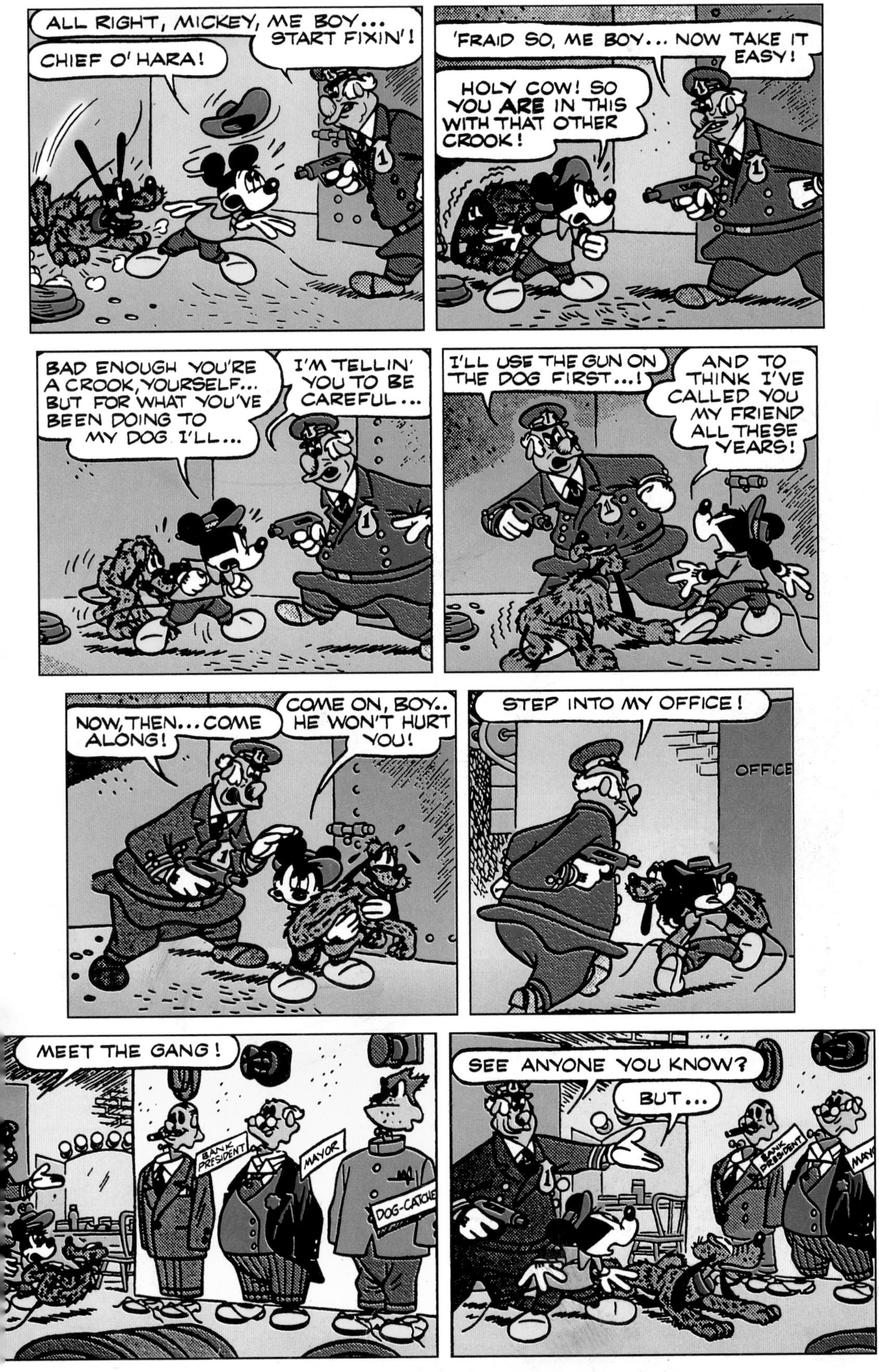
ALL RIGHT, MICKEY, ME BOY... START FIXIN'!
CHIEF O'HARA!
'FRAID SO, ME BOY... NOW TAKE IT EASY!
HOLY COW! SO YOU ARE IN THIS WITH THAT OTHER CROOK!
BAD ENOUGH YOU'RE A CROOK, YOURSELF... BUT FOR WHAT YOU'VE BEEN DOING TO MY DOG I'LL...
I'M TELLIN' YOU TO BE CAREFUL...
I'LL USE THE GUN ON THE DOG FIRST...!
AND TO THINK I'VE CALLED YOU MY FRIEND ALL THESE YEARS!
NOW, THEN... COME ALONG!
COME ON, BOY.. HE WON'T HURT YOU!
STEP INTO MY OFFICE!
OFFICE
MEET THE GANG!
BANK PRESIDENT
MAYOR
DOG-CATCHE
SEE ANYONE YOU KNOW?
BUT...
BANK PRESIDENT
MAYO

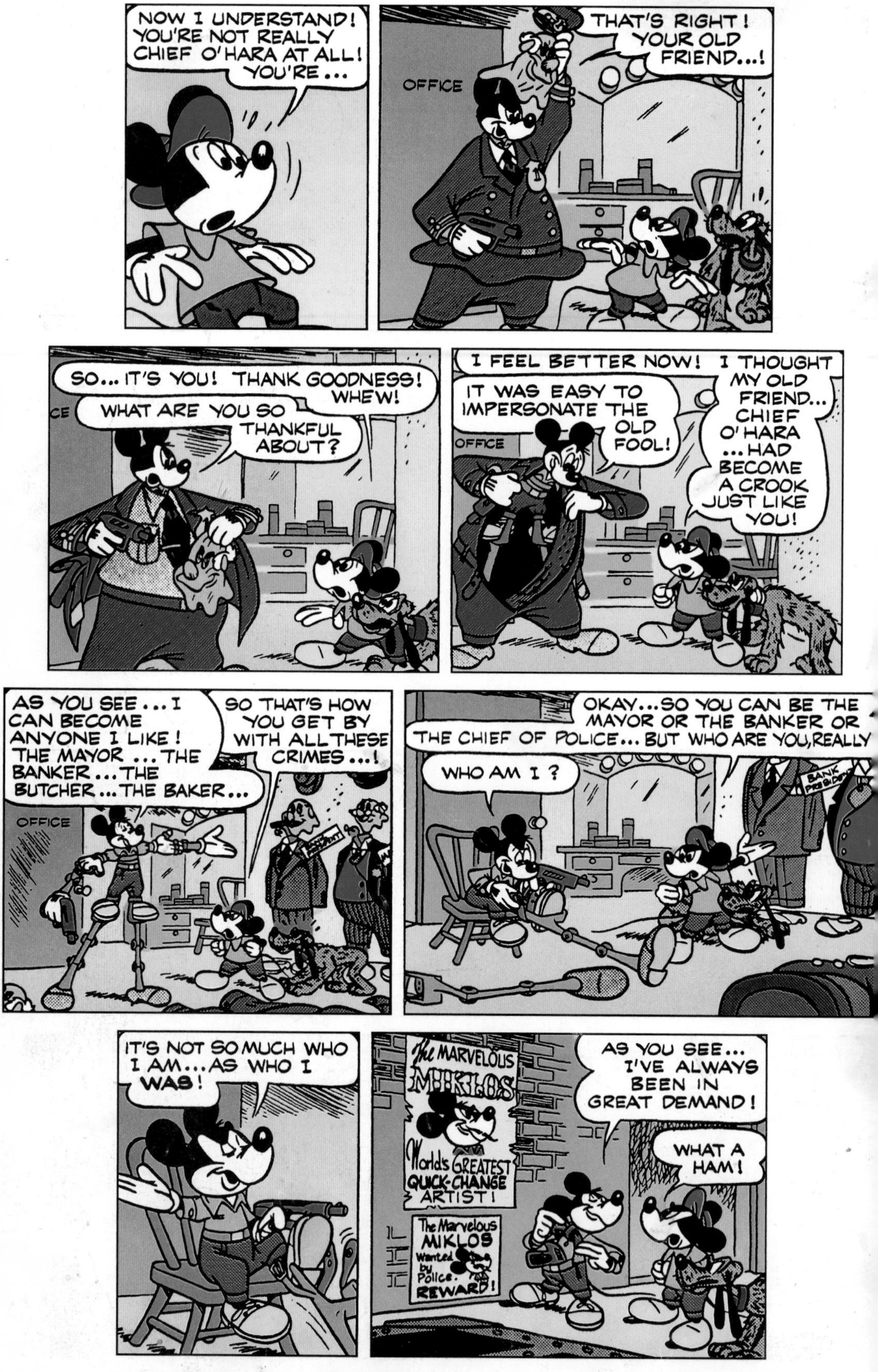
NOW I UNDERSTAND! YOU'RE NOT REALLY CHIEF O'HARA AT ALL! YOU'RE...
OFFICE
THAT'S RIGHT! YOUR OLD FRIEND...!
SO... IT'S YOU! THANK GOODNESS! WHEW!
WHAT ARE YOU SO THANKFUL ABOUT?
I FEEL BETTER NOW! I THOUGHT MY OLD FRIEND... CHIEF O'HARA ...HAD BECOME A CROOK JUST LIKE YOU!
IT WAS EASY TO IMPERSONATE THE OLD FOOL!
OFFICE
AS YOU SEE... I CAN BECOME ANYONE I LIKE! THE MAYOR ... THE BANKER... THE BUTCHER... THE BAKER...
SO THAT'S HOW YOU GET BY WITH ALL THESE CRIMES...!
OFFICE
OKAY... SO YOU CAN BE THE MAYOR OR THE BANKER OR THE CHIEF OF POLICE... BUT WHO ARE YOU, REALLY
WHO AM I?
IT'S NOT SO MUCH WHO I AM... AS WHO I WAS!
The MARVELOUS MIKLOS
World's GREATEST QUICK-CHANGE ARTIST!
The Marvelous MIKLOS Wanted by Police. REWARD!
AS YOU SEE... I'VE ALWAYS BEEN IN GREAT DEMAND!
WHAT A HAM!

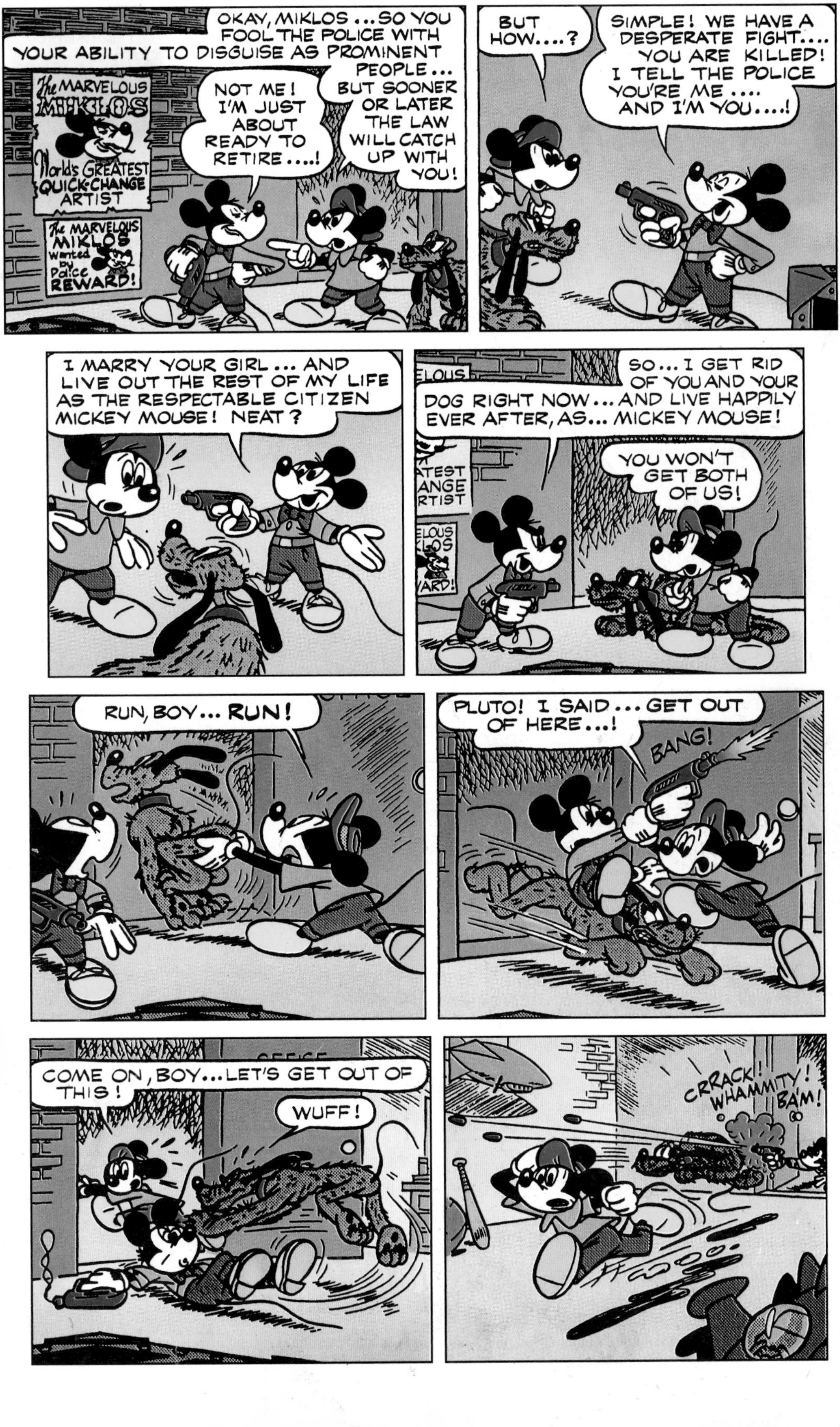
OKAY, MIKLOS ... SO YOU FOOL THE POLICE WITH YOUR ABILITY TO DISGUISE AS PROMINENT PEOPLE...
The MARVELOUS MIKLOS World's GREATEST QUICK-CHANGE ARTIST
The MARVELOUS MIKLOS Wanted by Police REWARD!
NOT ME! I'M JUST ABOUT READY TO RETIRE....!
BUT SOONER OR LATER THE LAW WILL CATCH UP WITH YOU!
BUT HOW....?
SIMPLE! WE HAVE A DESPERATE FIGHT.... YOU ARE KILLED! I TELL THE POLICE YOU'RE ME .... AND I'M YOU....!
I MARRY YOUR GIRL ... AND LIVE OUT THE REST OF MY LIFE AS THE RESPECTABLE CITIZEN MICKEY MOUSE! NEAT?
SO... I GET RID OF YOU AND YOUR DOG RIGHT NOW... AND LIVE HAPPILY EVER AFTER, AS... MICKEY MOUSE!
YOU WON'T GET BOTH OF US!
RUN, BOY... RUN!
PLUTO! I SAID... GET OUT OF HERE...!
BANG!
COME ON, BOY... LET'S GET OUT OF THIS!
WUFF!
CRRACK! WHAMMITY! BAM!

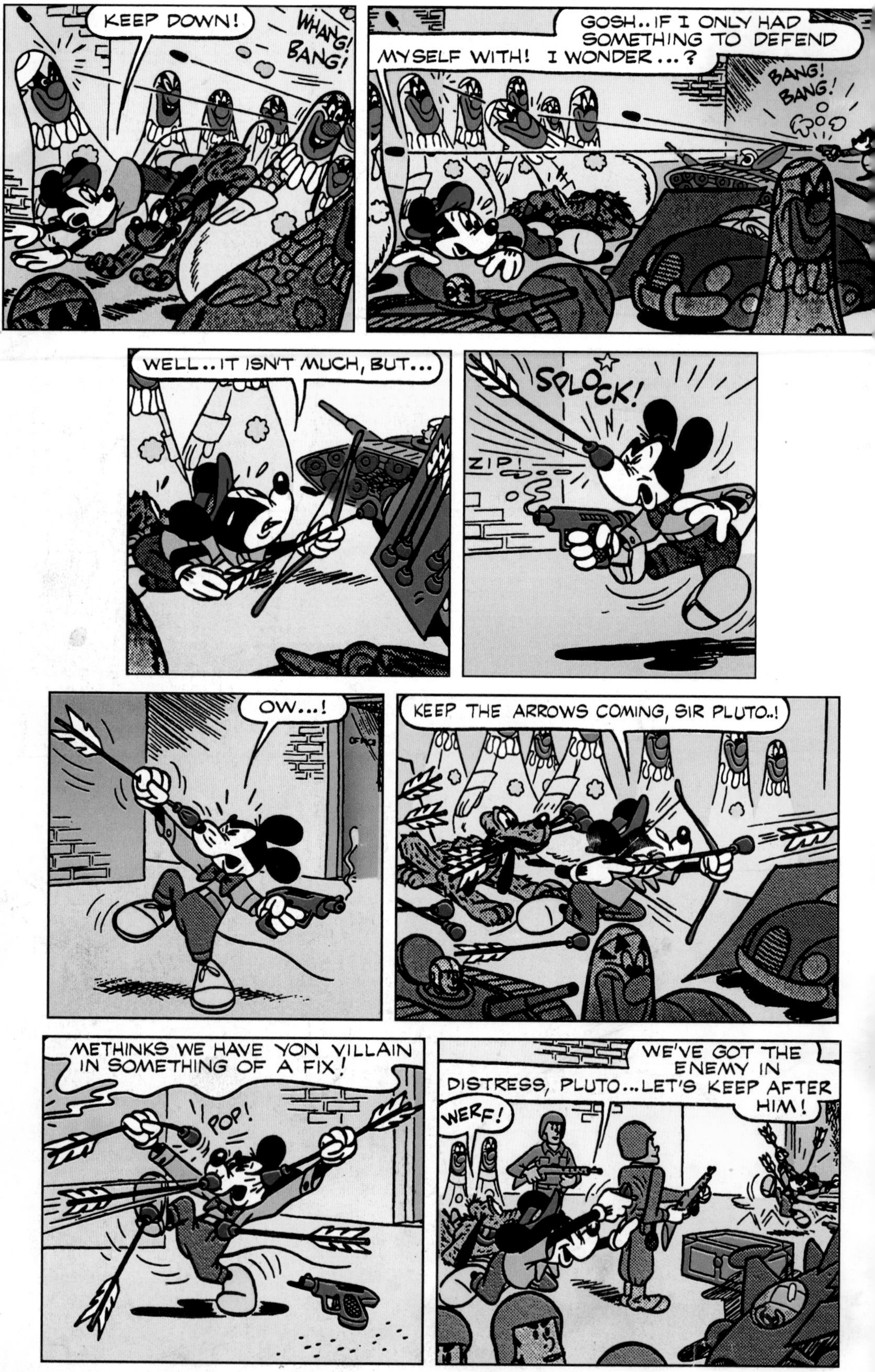
KEEP DOWN!
WHANG! BANG!
GOSH.. IF I ONLY HAD SOMETHING TO DEFEND MYSELF WITH! I WONDER...?
BANG! BANG!
WELL.. IT ISN'T MUCH, BUT...
SPLOCK!
ZIP!
OW...!
KEEP THE ARROWS COMING, SIR PLUTO..!
METHINKS WE HAVE YON VILLAIN IN SOMETHING OF A FIX!
POP!
WE'VE GOT THE ENEMY IN DISTRESS, PLUTO...LET'S KEEP AFTER HIM!
WERF!

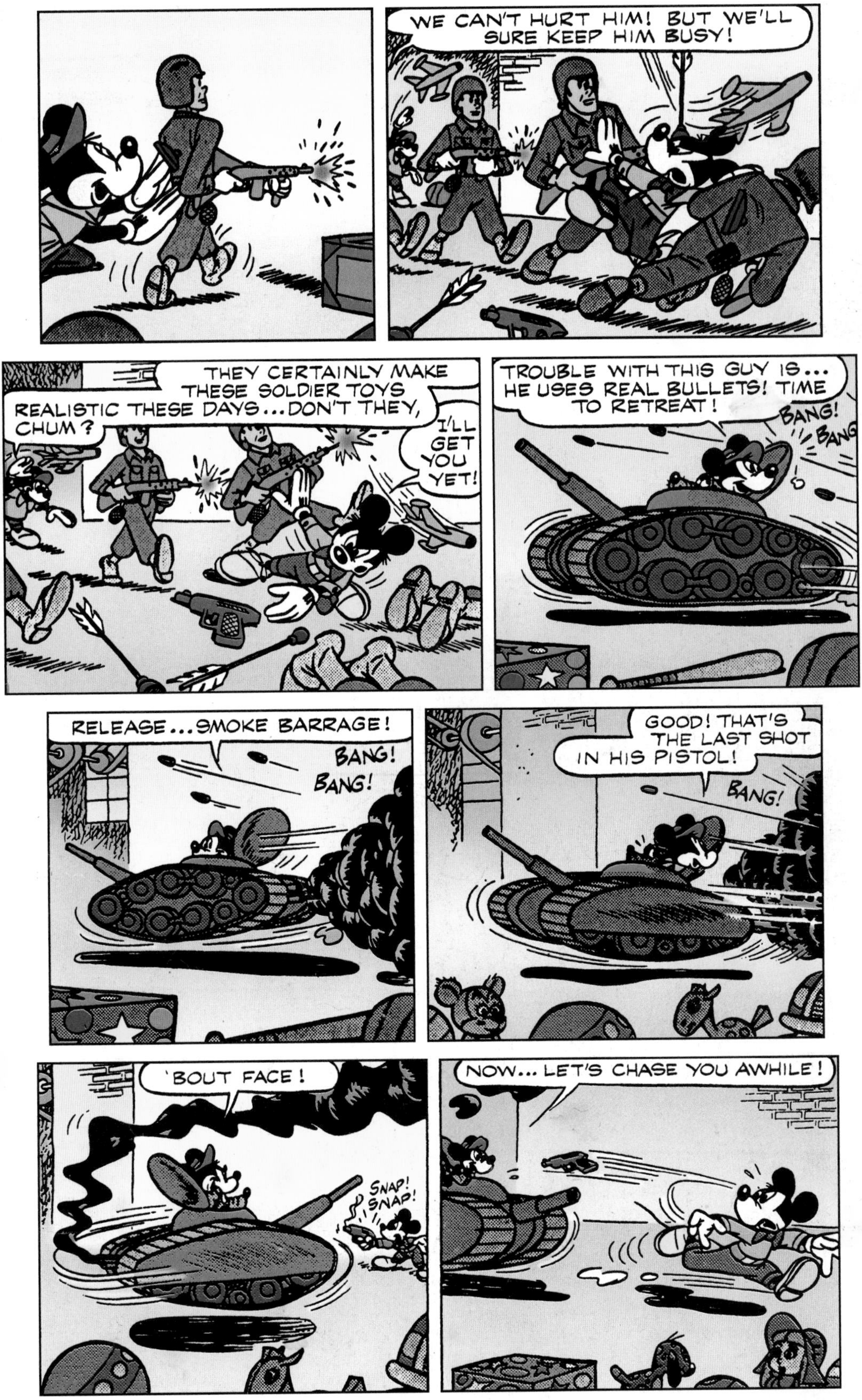
WE CAN'T HURT HIM! BUT WE'LL SURE KEEP HIM BUSY!
THEY CERTAINLY MAKE THESE SOLDIER TOYS REALISTIC THESE DAYS...DON'T THEY, CHUM?
I'LL GET YOU YET!
TROUBLE WITH THIS GUY IS... HE USES REAL BULLETS! TIME TO RETREAT!
BANG!
BANG
RELEASE...SMOKE BARRAGE!
BANG!
BANG!
GOOD! THAT'S THE LAST SHOT IN HIS PISTOL!
BANG!
'BOUT FACE!
SNAP! SNAP!
NOW... LET'S CHASE YOU AWHILE!

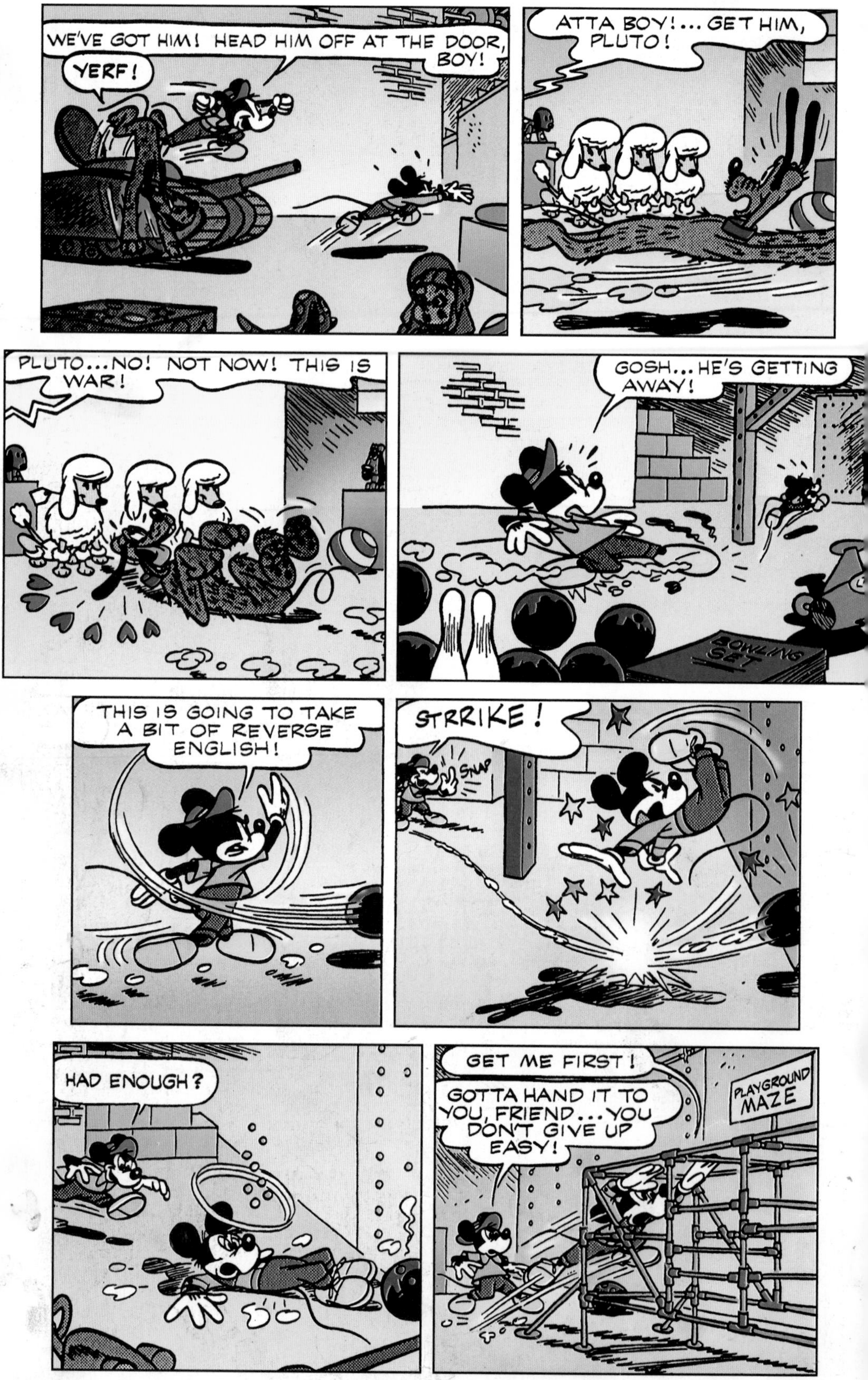
WE'VE GOT HIM! HEAD HIM OFF AT THE DOOR, BOY!
YERF!
ATTA BOY!... GET HIM, PLUTO!
PLUTO...NO! NOT NOW! THIS IS WAR!
GOSH... HE'S GETTING AWAY!
BOWLING SET
THIS IS GOING TO TAKE A BIT OF REVERSE ENGLISH!
STRRIKE!
SNAP
HAD ENOUGH?
GET ME FIRST!
GOTTA HAND IT TO YOU, FRIEND... YOU DON'T GIVE UP EASY!
PLAYGROUND MAZE

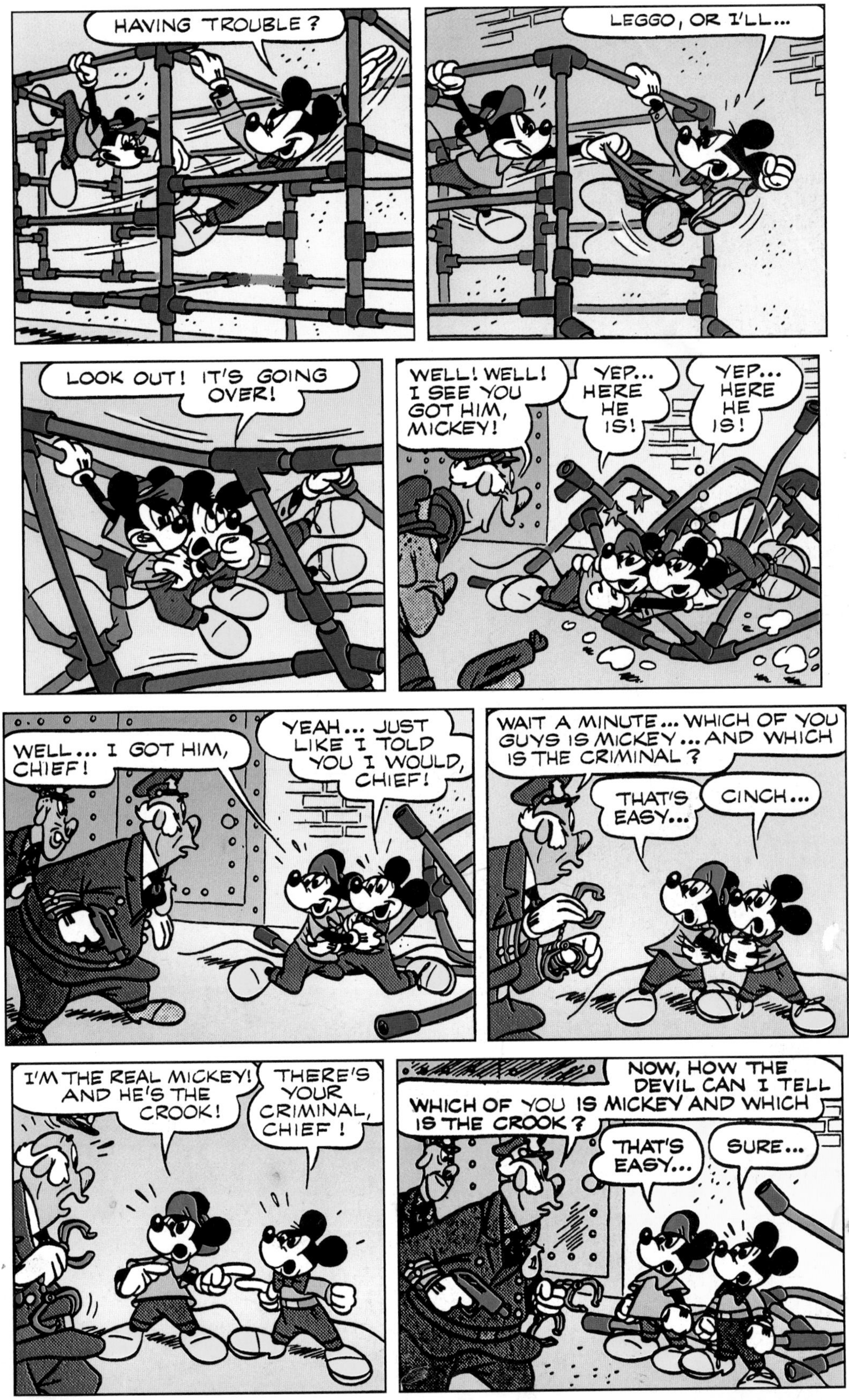

HAVING TROUBLE?
LEGGO, OR I'LL...
LOOK OUT! IT'S GOING OVER!
WELL! WELL! I SEE YOU GOT HIM, MICKEY!
YEP... HERE HE IS!
YEP... HERE HE IS!
WELL... I GOT HIM, CHIEF!
YEAH... JUST LIKE I TOLD YOU I WOULD, CHIEF!
WAIT A MINUTE... WHICH OF YOU GUYS IS MICKEY... AND WHICH IS THE CRIMINAL?
THAT'S EASY...
CINCH...
I'M THE REAL MICKEY! AND HE'S THE CROOK!
THERE'S YOUR CRIMINAL, CHIEF!
NOW, HOW THE DEVIL CAN I TELL WHICH OF YOU IS MICKEY AND WHICH IS THE CROOK?
THAT'S EASY...
SURE...

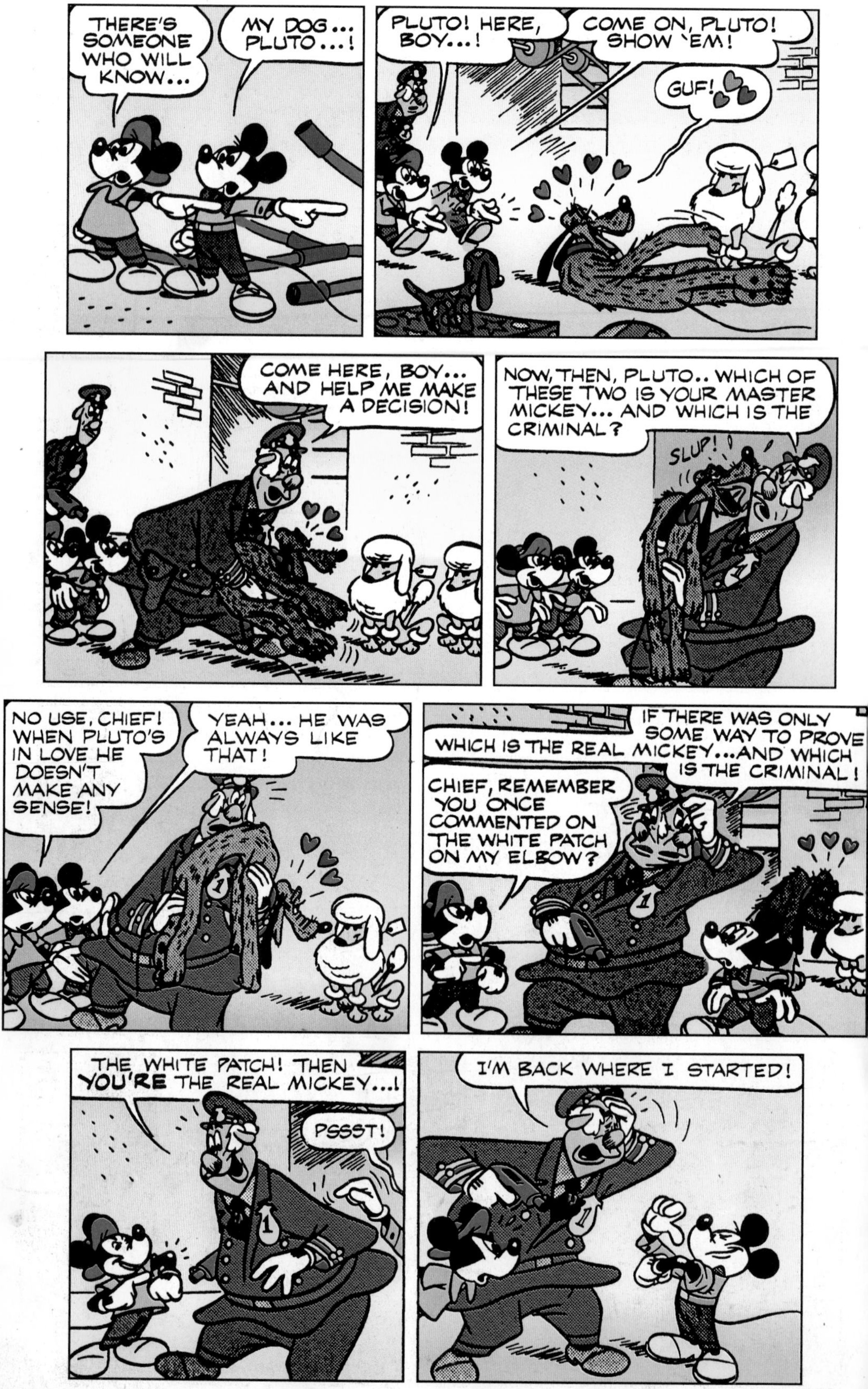
THERE'S SOMEONE WHO WILL KNOW...
MY DOG... PLUTO...!
PLUTO! HERE, BOY...!
COME ON, PLUTO! SHOW 'EM!
GUF!
COME HERE, BOY... AND HELP ME MAKE A DECISION!
NOW, THEN, PLUTO.. WHICH OF THESE TWO IS YOUR MASTER MICKEY... AND WHICH IS THE CRIMINAL?
SLUP!
NO USE, CHIEF! WHEN PLUTO'S IN LOVE HE DOESN'T MAKE ANY SENSE!
YEAH... HE WAS ALWAYS LIKE THAT!
IF THERE WAS ONLY SOME WAY TO PROVE WHICH IS THE REAL MICKEY...AND WHICH IS THE CRIMINAL!
CHIEF, REMEMBER YOU ONCE COMMENTED ON THE WHITE PATCH ON MY ELBOW?
THE WHITE PATCH! THEN YOU'RE THE REAL MICKEY...!
PSSST!
I'M BACK WHERE I STARTED!

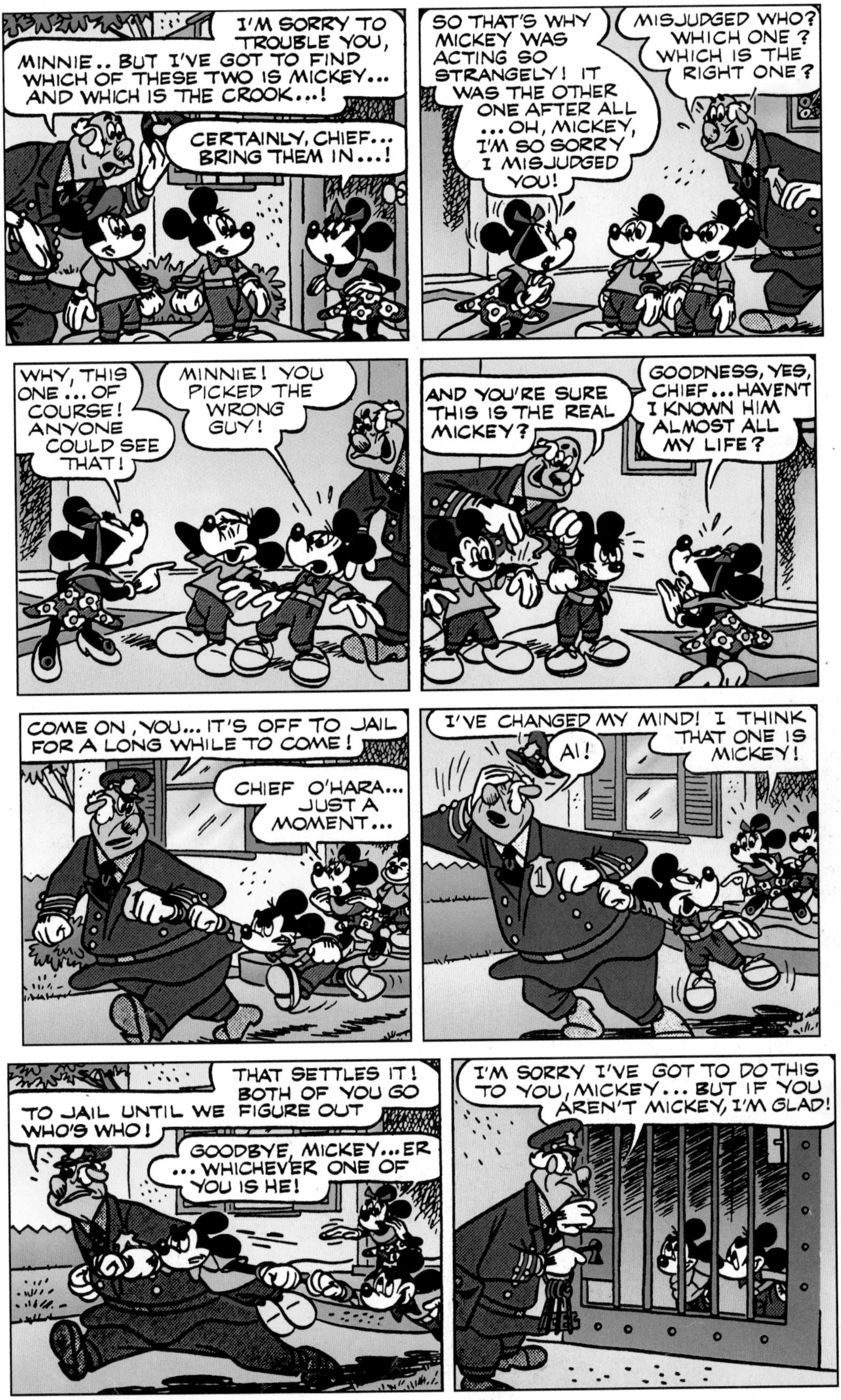
I'M SORRY TO TROUBLE YOU, MINNIE.. BUT I'VE GOT TO FIND WHICH OF THESE TWO IS MICKEY... AND WHICH IS THE CROOK...!
CERTAINLY, CHIEF... BRING THEM IN...!
SO THAT'S WHY MICKEY WAS ACTING SO STRANGELY! IT WAS THE OTHER ONE AFTER ALL ...OH, MICKEY, I'M SO SORRY I MISJUDGED YOU!
MISJUDGED WHO? WHICH ONE? WHICH IS THE RIGHT ONE?
WHY, THIS ONE... OF COURSE! ANYONE COULD SEE THAT!
MINNIE! YOU PICKED THE WRONG GUY!
AND YOU'RE SURE THIS IS THE REAL MICKEY?
GOODNESS, YES, CHIEF... HAVEN'T I KNOWN HIM ALMOST ALL MY LIFE?
COME ON, YOU... IT'S OFF TO JAIL FOR A LONG WHILE TO COME!
CHIEF O'HARA... JUST A MOMENT...
I'VE CHANGED MY MIND! I THINK THAT ONE IS MICKEY!
AI!
THAT SETTLES IT! BOTH OF YOU GO TO JAIL UNTIL WE FIGURE OUT WHO'S WHO!
GOODBYE, MICKEY...ER ...WHICHEVER ONE OF YOU IS HE!
I'M SORRY I'VE GOT TO DO THIS TO YOU, MICKEY... BUT IF YOU AREN'T MICKEY, I'M GLAD!
1

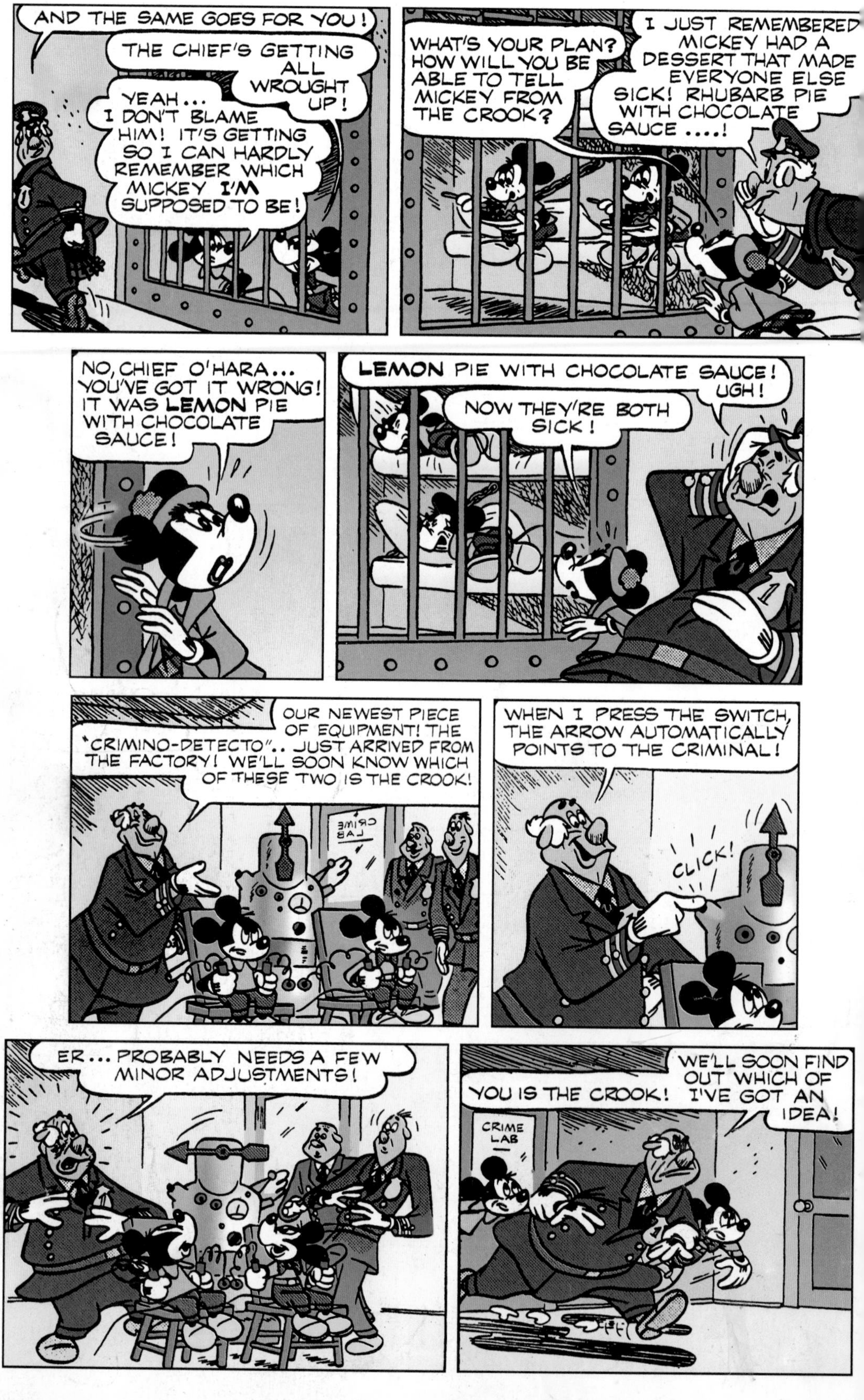
AND THE SAME GOES FOR YOU!
THE CHIEF'S GETTING ALL WROUGHT UP!
YEAH... I DON'T BLAME HIM! IT'S GETTING SO I CAN HARDLY REMEMBER WHICH MICKEY I'M SUPPOSED TO BE!
WHAT'S YOUR PLAN? HOW WILL YOU BE ABLE TO TELL MICKEY FROM THE CROOK?
I JUST REMEMBERED MICKEY HAD A DESSERT THAT MADE EVERYONE ELSE SICK! RHUBARB PIE WITH CHOCOLATE SAUCE ....!
NO, CHIEF O'HARA... YOU'VE GOT IT WRONG! IT WAS LEMON PIE WITH CHOCOLATE SAUCE!
LEMON PIE WITH CHOCOLATE SAUCE! UGH!
NOW THEY'RE BOTH SICK!
OUR NEWEST PIECE OF EQUIPMENT! THE "CRIMINO-DETECTO".. JUST ARRIVED FROM THE FACTORY! WE'LL SOON KNOW WHICH OF THESE TWO IS THE CROOK!
CRIME LAB
WHEN I PRESS THE SWITCH, THE ARROW AUTOMATICALLY POINTS TO THE CRIMINAL!
CLICK!
ER... PROBABLY NEEDS A FEW MINOR ADJUSTMENTS!
CRIME LAB
WE'LL SOON FIND OUT WHICH OF YOU IS THE CROOK! I'VE GOT AN IDEA!

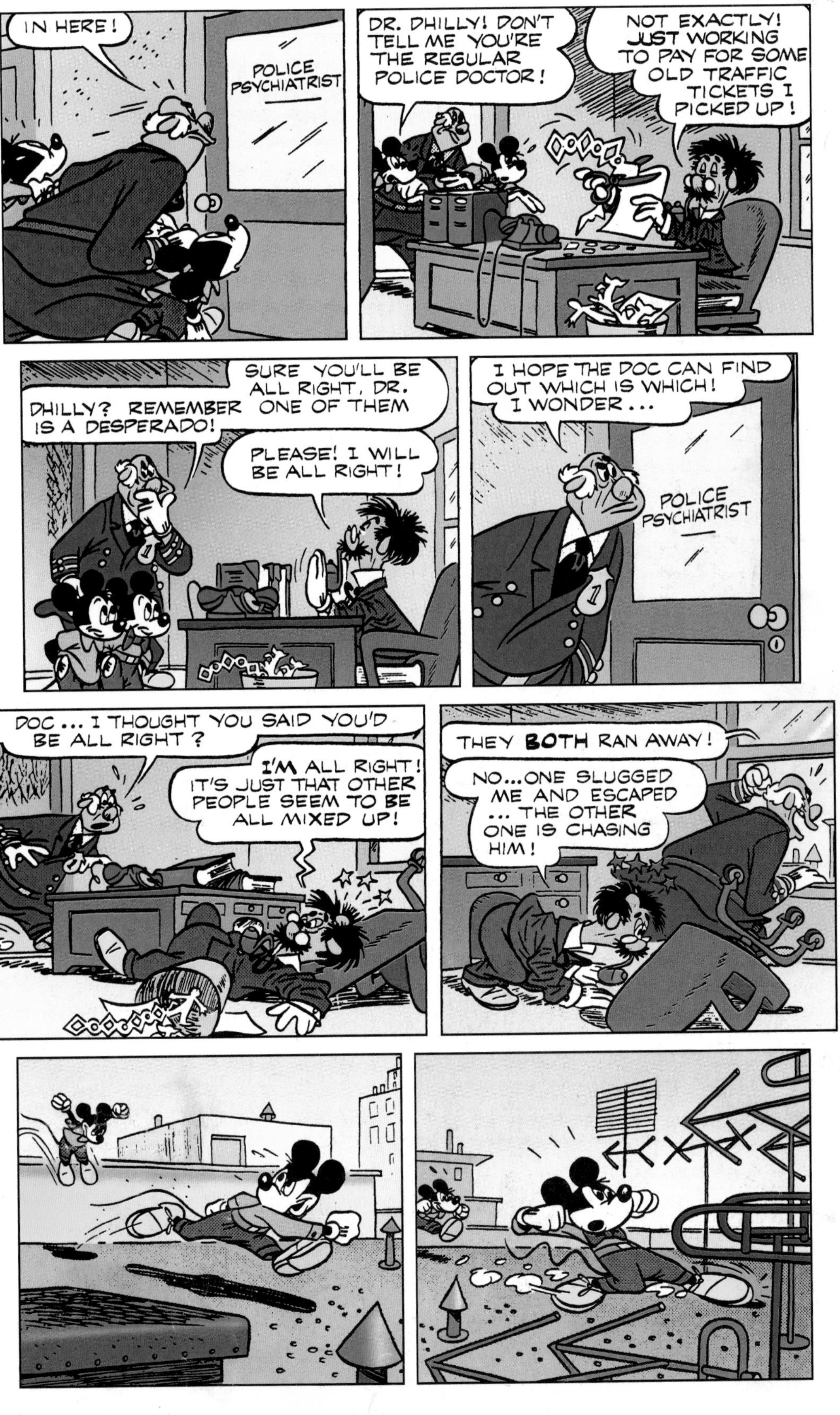
IN HERE!
POLICE PSYCHIATRIST
DR. DHILLY! DON'T TELL ME YOU'RE THE REGULAR POLICE DOCTOR!
NOT EXACTLY! JUST WORKING TO PAY FOR SOME OLD TRAFFIC TICKETS I PICKED UP!
SURE YOU'LL BE ALL RIGHT, DR. DHILLY? REMEMBER ONE OF THEM IS A DESPERADO!
PLEASE! I WILL BE ALL RIGHT!
I HOPE THE DOC CAN FIND OUT WHICH IS WHICH! I WONDER...
POLICE PSYCHIATRIST
DOC... I THOUGHT YOU SAID YOU'D BE ALL RIGHT?
I'M ALL RIGHT! IT'S JUST THAT OTHER PEOPLE SEEM TO BE ALL MIXED UP!
THEY BOTH RAN AWAY!
NO...ONE SLUGGED ME AND ESCAPED ... THE OTHER ONE IS CHASING HIM!

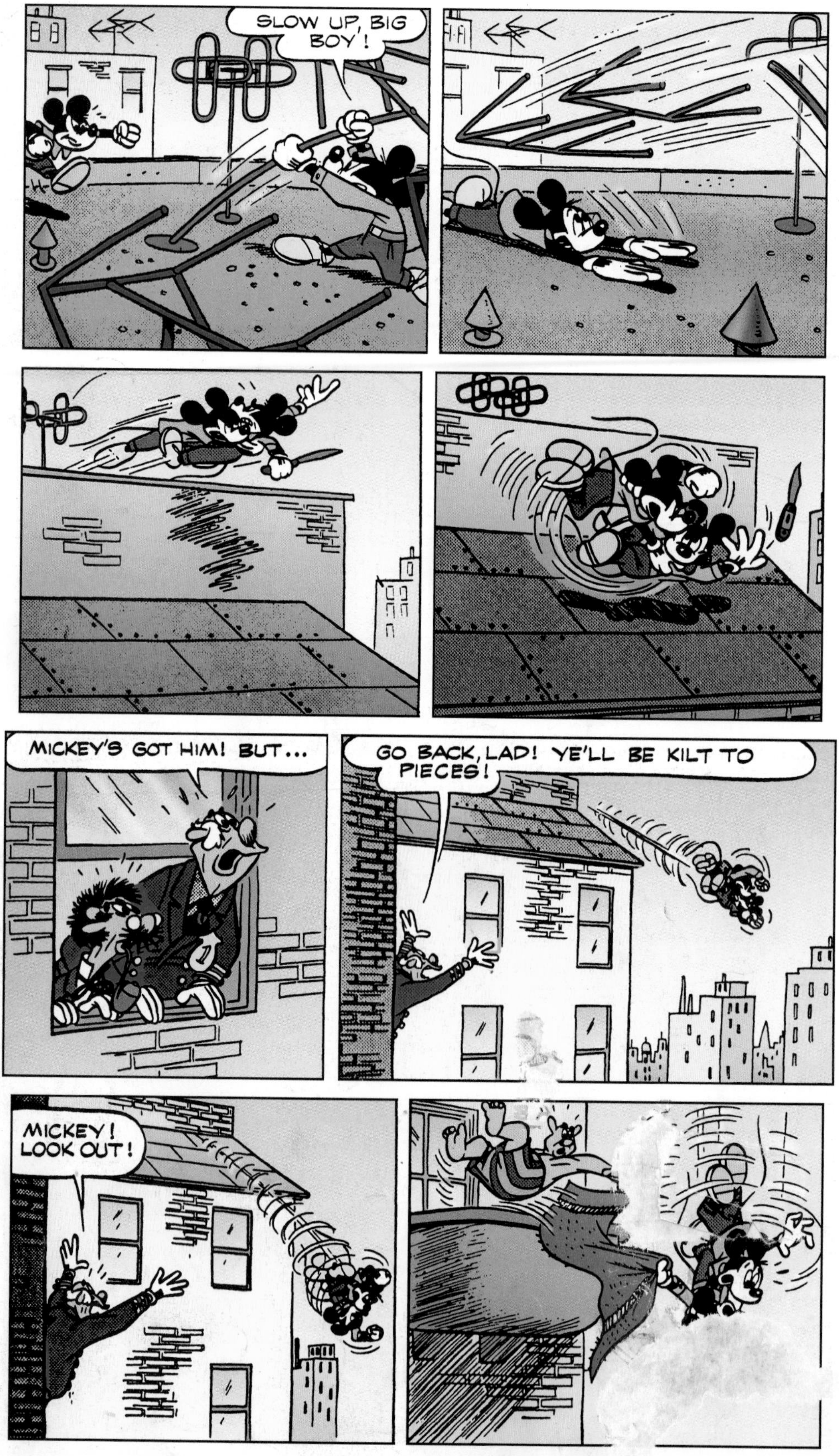
SLOW UP, BIG BOY!
MICKEY'S GOT HIM! BUT...
GO BACK, LAD! YE'LL BE KILT TO PIECES!
MICKEY! LOOK OUT!

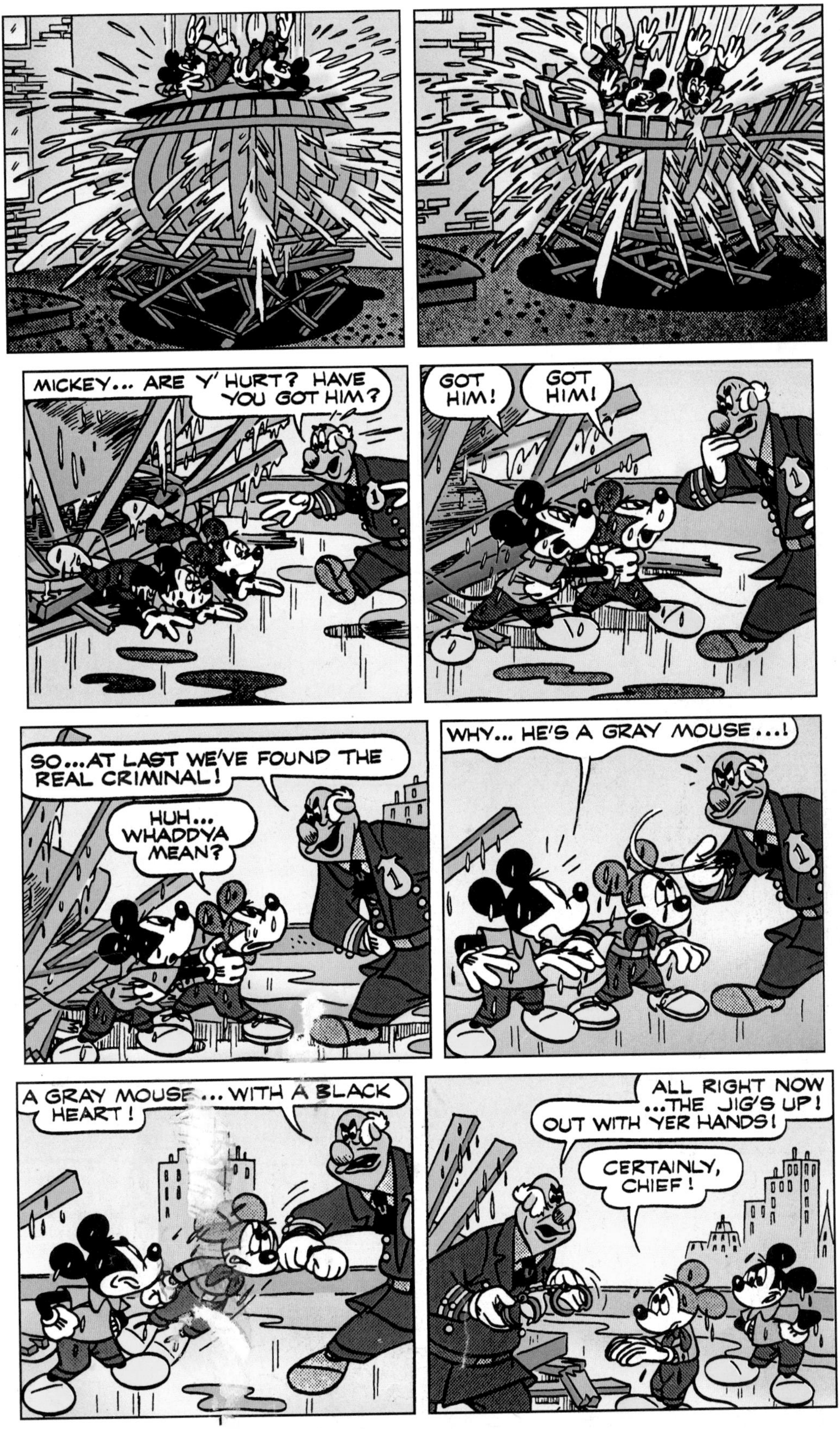
MICKEY... ARE Y' HURT? HAVE YOU GOT HIM?
GOT HIM!
GOT HIM!
SO...AT LAST WE'VE FOUND THE REAL CRIMINAL!
HUH... WHADDYA MEAN?
WHY... HE'S A GRAY MOUSE...!
A GRAY MOUSE... WITH A BLACK HEART!
ALL RIGHT NOW ...THE JIG'S UP! OUT WITH YER HANDS!
CERTAINLY, CHIEF!

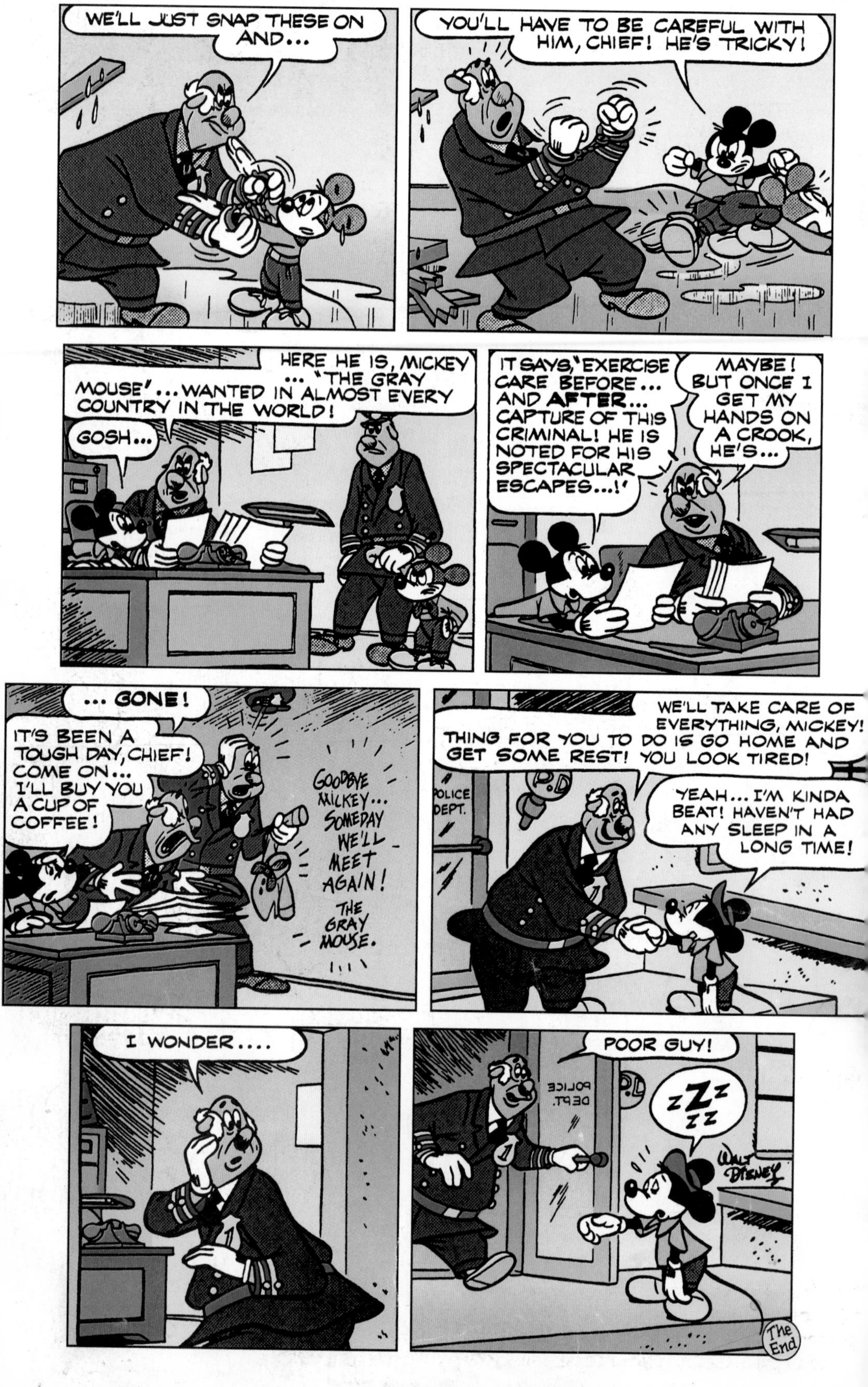
WE'LL JUST SNAP THESE ON AND...
YOU'LL HAVE TO BE CAREFUL WITH HIM, CHIEF! HE'S TRICKY!
HERE HE IS, MICKEY ... "THE GRAY MOUSE"... WANTED IN ALMOST EVERY COUNTRY IN THE WORLD!
GOSH...
IT SAYS, "EXERCISE CARE BEFORE... AND AFTER... CAPTURE OF THIS CRIMINAL! HE IS NOTED FOR HIS SPECTACULAR ESCAPES...!"
MAYBE! BUT ONCE I GET MY HANDS ON A CROOK, HE'S...
... GONE!
IT'S BEEN A TOUGH DAY, CHIEF! COME ON... I'LL BUY YOU A CUP OF COFFEE!
GOODBYE MICKEY... SOMEDAY WE'LL MEET AGAIN! THE GRAY MOUSE.
WE'LL TAKE CARE OF EVERYTHING, MICKEY! THING FOR YOU TO DO IS GO HOME AND GET SOME REST! YOU LOOK TIRED!
POLICE DEPT.
YEAH... I'M KINDA BEAT! HAVEN'T HAD ANY SLEEP IN A LONG TIME!
I WONDER....
POOR GUY!
ZZZ ZZ
WALT DISNEY
The End

Uncle Scrooge is in another bind. Can Donald and the boys save him from the Peeweegahs? ("What's a Peeweegah," you ask?)

UH OH!

©2007 Disney Enterprises, In

Learn all about Peeweegahs and Wendigos in *Walt Disney's Uncle Scrooge Adventures—The Barks/Rosa Collection*. This new series features stories by famed writers/illustrators Carl Barks and Don Rosa. Each volume contains an original Carl Barks classic followed by a Don Rosa sequel. Volume One kicks things off with "Land of the Pygmy Indians" and "War of the Wendigo."

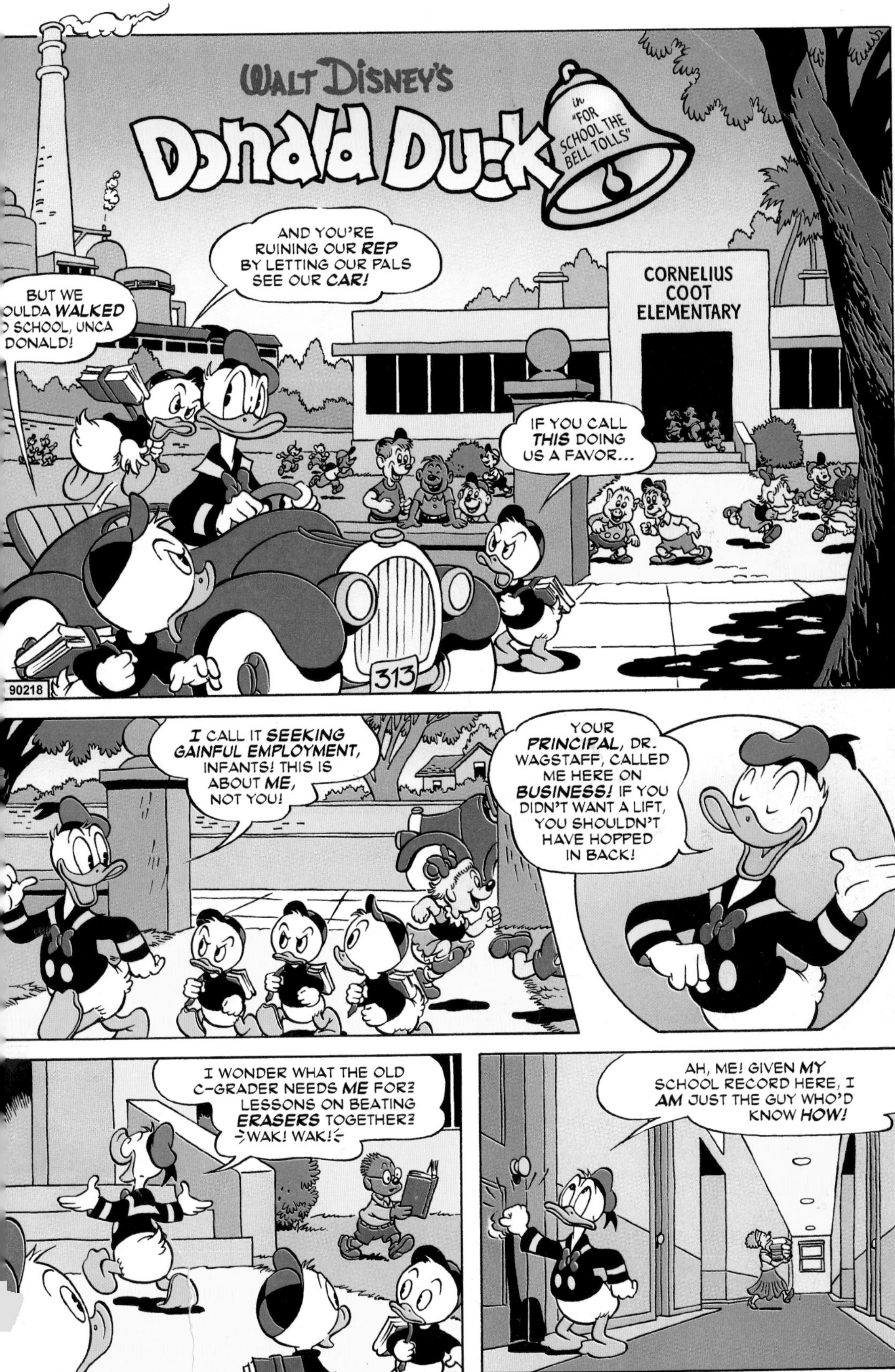
WALT DISNEY'S
Donald Duck
in "FOR SCHOOL THE BELL TOLLS"
BUT WE
OULDA WALKED
SCHOOL, UNCA
DONALD!
AND YOU'RE RUINING OUR REP BY LETTING OUR PALS SEE OUR CAR!
CORNELIUS COOT ELEMENTARY
IF YOU CALL THIS DOING US A FAVOR...
313
90218
I CALL IT SEEKING GAINFUL EMPLOYMENT, INFANTS! THIS IS ABOUT ME, NOT YOU!
YOUR PRINCIPAL, DR. WAGSTAFF, CALLED ME HERE ON BUSINESS! IF YOU DIDN'T WANT A LIFT, YOU SHOULDN'T HAVE HOPPED IN BACK!
I WONDER WHAT THE OLD C-GRADER NEEDS ME FOR? LESSONS ON BEATING ERASERS TOGETHER? WAK! WAK!
AH, ME! GIVEN MY SCHOOL RECORD HERE, I AM JUST THE GUY WHO'D KNOW HOW!

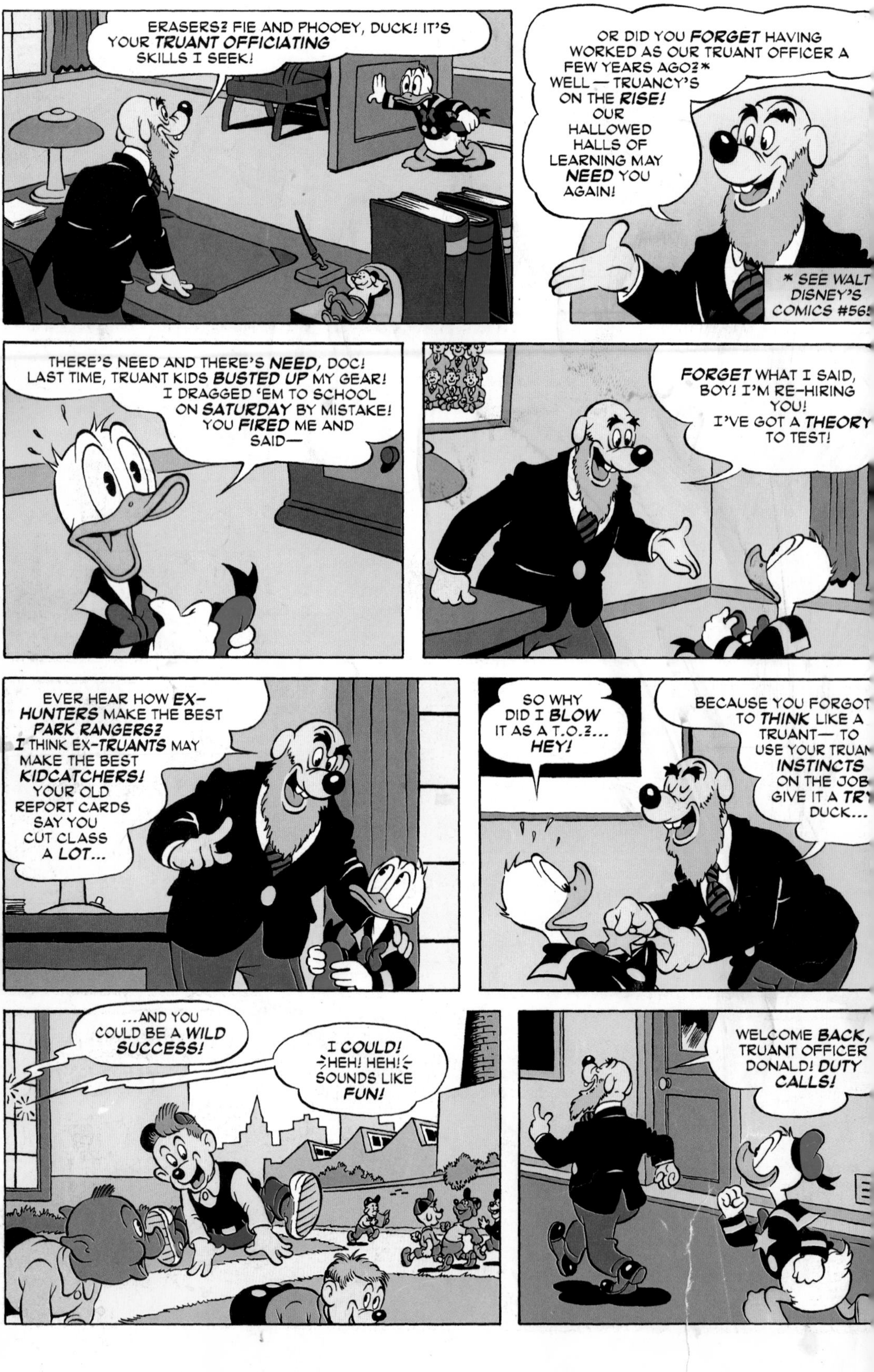
ERASERS? FIE AND PHOOEY, DUCK! IT'S YOUR TRUANT OFFICIATING SKILLS I SEEK!
OR DID YOU FORGET HAVING WORKED AS OUR TRUANT OFFICER A FEW YEARS AGO?* WELL — TRUANCY'S ON THE RISE! OUR HALLOWED HALLS OF LEARNING MAY NEED YOU AGAIN!
* SEE WALT DISNEY'S COMICS #56!
THERE'S NEED AND THERE'S NEED, DOC! LAST TIME, TRUANT KIDS BUSTED UP MY GEAR! I DRAGGED 'EM TO SCHOOL ON SATURDAY BY MISTAKE! YOU FIRED ME AND SAID—
FORGET WHAT I SAID, BOY! I'M RE-HIRING YOU! I'VE GOT A THEORY TO TEST!
EVER HEAR HOW EX-HUNTERS MAKE THE BEST PARK RANGERS? I THINK EX-TRUANTS MAY MAKE THE BEST KIDCATCHERS! YOUR OLD REPORT CARDS SAY YOU CUT CLASS A LOT...
SO WHY DID I BLOW IT AS A T.O.?... HEY!
BECAUSE YOU FORGOT TO THINK LIKE A TRUANT— TO USE YOUR TRUANT INSTINCTS ON THE JOB. GIVE IT A TRY, DUCK...
...AND YOU COULD BE A WILD SUCCESS!
I COULD! HEH! HEH! SOUNDS LIKE FUN!
WELCOME BACK, TRUANT OFFICER DONALD! DUTY CALLS!

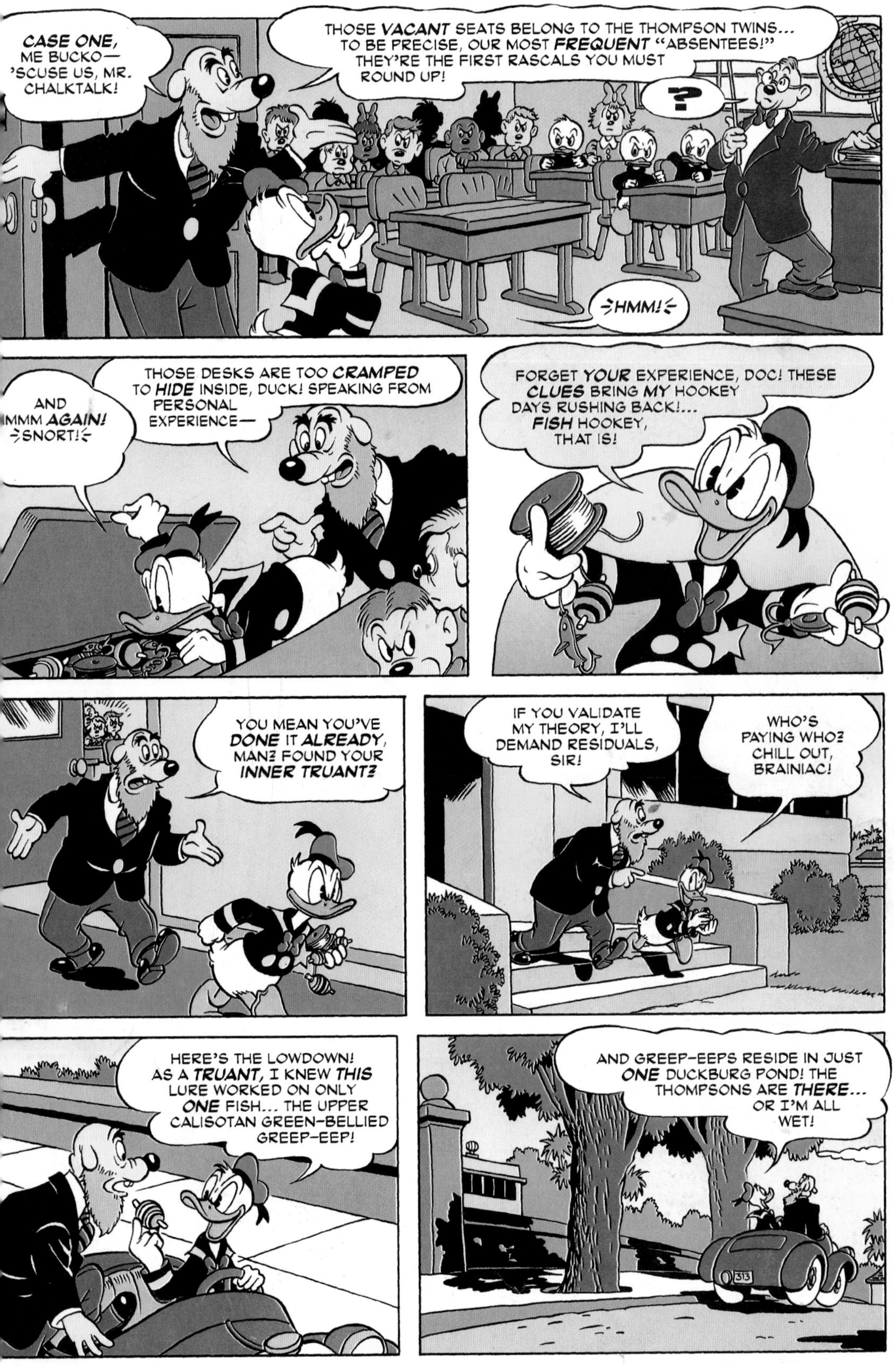
CASE ONE, ME BUCKO— 'SCUSE US, MR. CHALKTALK!
THOSE VACANT SEATS BELONG TO THE THOMPSON TWINS... TO BE PRECISE, OUR MOST FREQUENT "ABSENTEES!" THEY'RE THE FIRST RASCALS YOU MUST ROUND UP!
?
HMM!
AND MMM AGAIN! SNORT!
THOSE DESKS ARE TOO CRAMPED TO HIDE INSIDE, DUCK! SPEAKING FROM PERSONAL EXPERIENCE—
FORGET YOUR EXPERIENCE, DOC! THESE CLUES BRING MY HOOKEY DAYS RUSHING BACK!... FISH HOOKEY, THAT IS!
YOU MEAN YOU'VE DONE IT ALREADY, MAN? FOUND YOUR INNER TRUANT?
IF YOU VALIDATE MY THEORY, I'LL DEMAND RESIDUALS, SIR!
WHO'S PAYING WHO? CHILL OUT, BRAINIAC!
HERE'S THE LOWDOWN! AS A TRUANT, I KNEW THIS LURE WORKED ON ONLY ONE FISH... THE UPPER CALISOTAN GREEN-BELLIED GREEP-EEP!
AND GREEP-EEPS RESIDE IN JUST ONE DUCKBURG POND! THE THOMPSONS ARE THERE... OR I'M ALL WET!
313

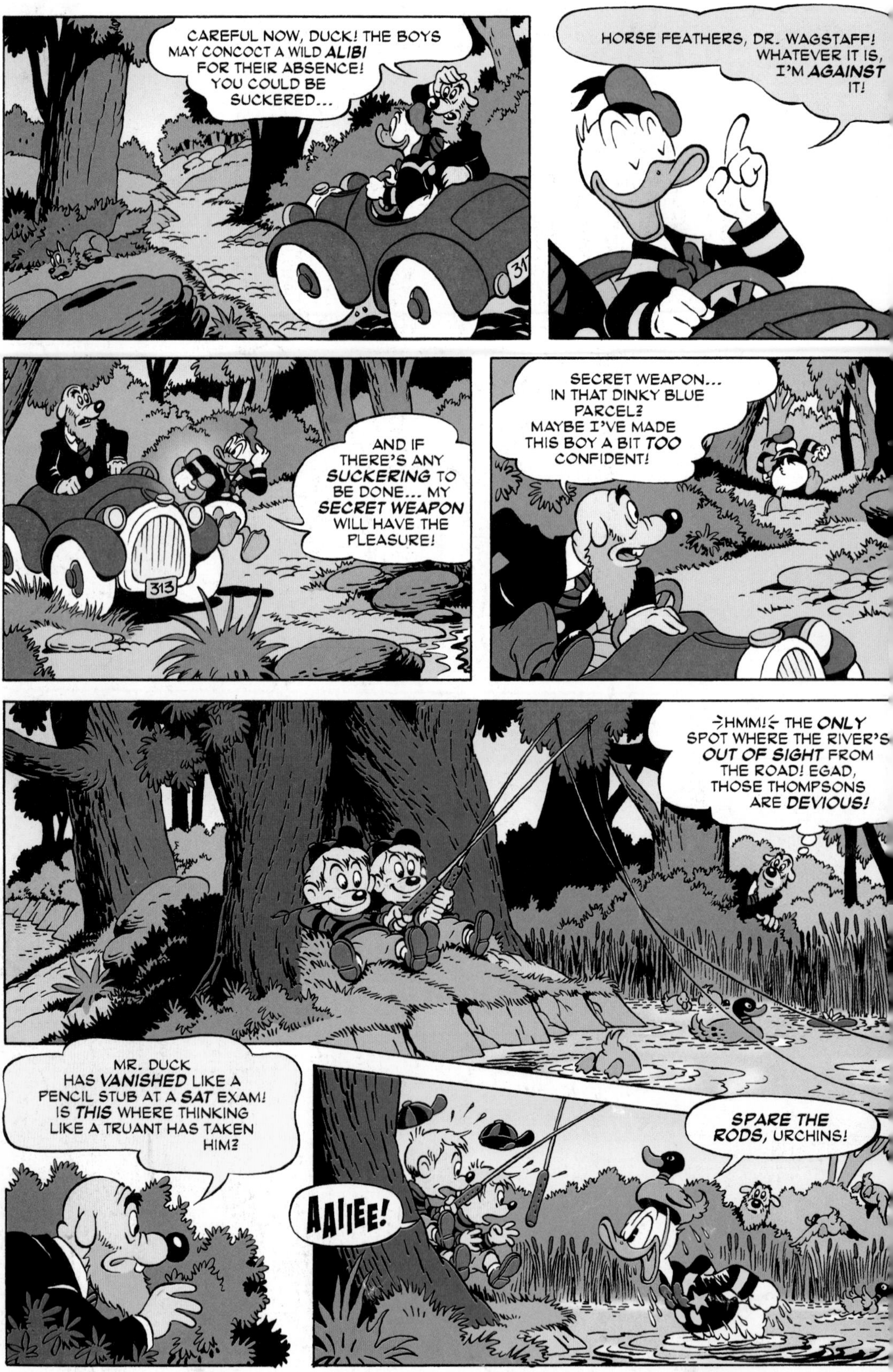
CAREFUL NOW, DUCK! THE BOYS MAY CONCOCT A WILD ALIBI FOR THEIR ABSENCE! YOU COULD BE SUCKERED...
HORSE FEATHERS, DR. WAGSTAFF! WHATEVER IT IS, I'M AGAINST IT!
AND IF THERE'S ANY SUCKERING TO BE DONE... MY SECRET WEAPON WILL HAVE THE PLEASURE!
SECRET WEAPON... IN THAT DINKY BLUE PARCEL? MAYBE I'VE MADE THIS BOY A BIT TOO CONFIDENT!
HMM! THE ONLY SPOT WHERE THE RIVER'S OUT OF SIGHT FROM THE ROAD! EGAD, THOSE THOMPSONS ARE DEVIOUS!
MR. DUCK HAS VANISHED LIKE A PENCIL STUB AT A SAT EXAM! IS THIS WHERE THINKING LIKE A TRUANT HAS TAKEN HIM?
AAIIEE!
SPARE THE RODS, URCHINS!

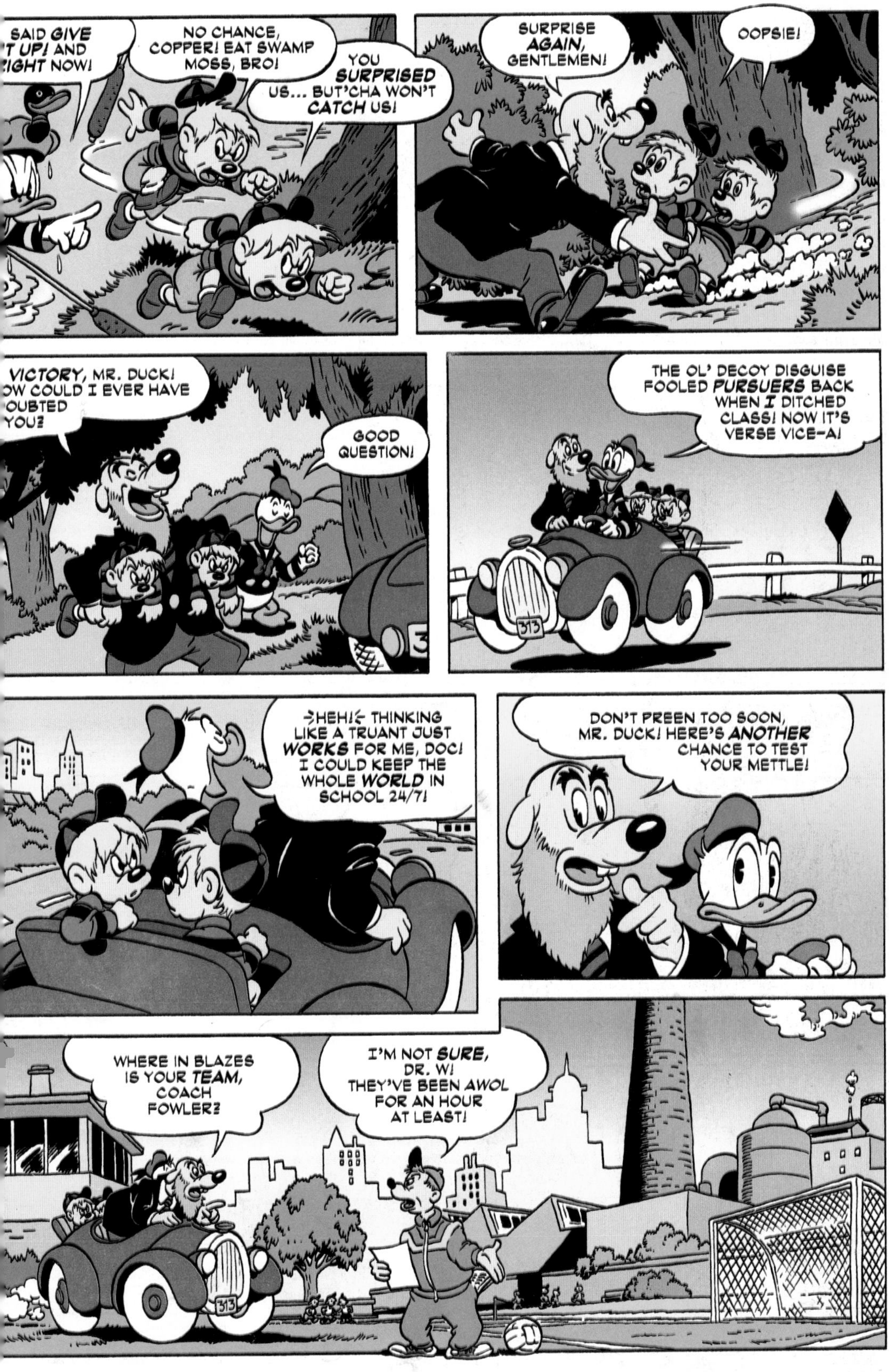

SAID GIVE
T UP! AND
IGHT NOW!
NO CHANCE, COPPER! EAT SWAMP MOSS, BRO!
YOU SURPRISED US... BUT'CHA WON'T CATCH US!
SURPRISE AGAIN, GENTLEMEN!
OOPSIE!
VICTORY, MR. DUCK!
OW COULD I EVER HAVE
OUBTED
YOU?
GOOD QUESTION!
THE OL' DECOY DISGUISE FOOLED PURSUERS BACK WHEN I DITCHED CLASS! NOW IT'S VERSE VICE-A!
HEH! THINKING LIKE A TRUANT JUST WORKS FOR ME, DOC! I COULD KEEP THE WHOLE WORLD IN SCHOOL 24/7!
DON'T PREEN TOO SOON, MR. DUCK! HERE'S ANOTHER CHANCE TO TEST YOUR METTLE!
WHERE IN BLAZES IS YOUR TEAM, COACH FOWLER?
I'M NOT SURE, DR. W! THEY'VE BEEN AWOL FOR AN HOUR AT LEAST!
313

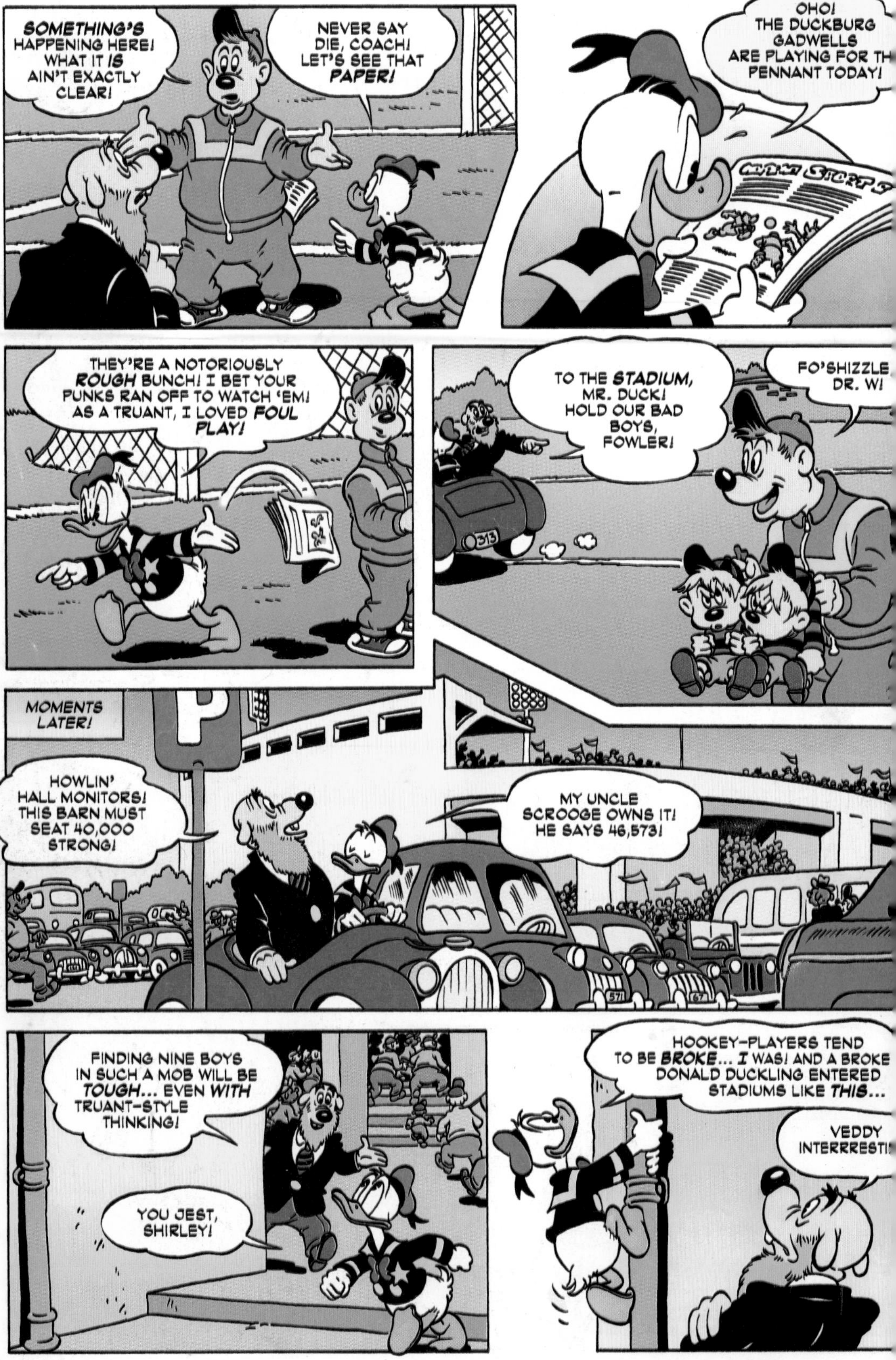
SOMETHING'S HAPPENING HERE! WHAT IT IS AIN'T EXACTLY CLEAR!
NEVER SAY DIE, COACH! LET'S SEE THAT PAPER!
OHO! THE DUCKBURG GADWELLS ARE PLAYING FOR TH PENNANT TODAY!
THEY'RE A NOTORIOUSLY ROUGH BUNCH! I BET YOUR PUNKS RAN OFF TO WATCH 'EM! AS A TRUANT, I LOVED FOUL PLAY!
TO THE STADIUM, MR. DUCK! HOLD OUR BAD BOYS, FOWLER!
FO'SHIZZLE DR. W!
MOMENTS LATER!
HOWLIN' HALL MONITORS! THIS BARN MUST SEAT 40,000 STRONG!
MY UNCLE SCROOGE OWNS IT! HE SAYS 46,573!
FINDING NINE BOYS IN SUCH A MOB WILL BE TOUGH... EVEN WITH TRUANT-STYLE THINKING!
YOU JEST, SHIRLEY!
HOOKEY-PLAYERS TEND TO BE BROKE... I WAS! AND A BROKE DONALD DUCKLING ENTERED STADIUMS LIKE THIS...
VEDDY INTERRRESTI

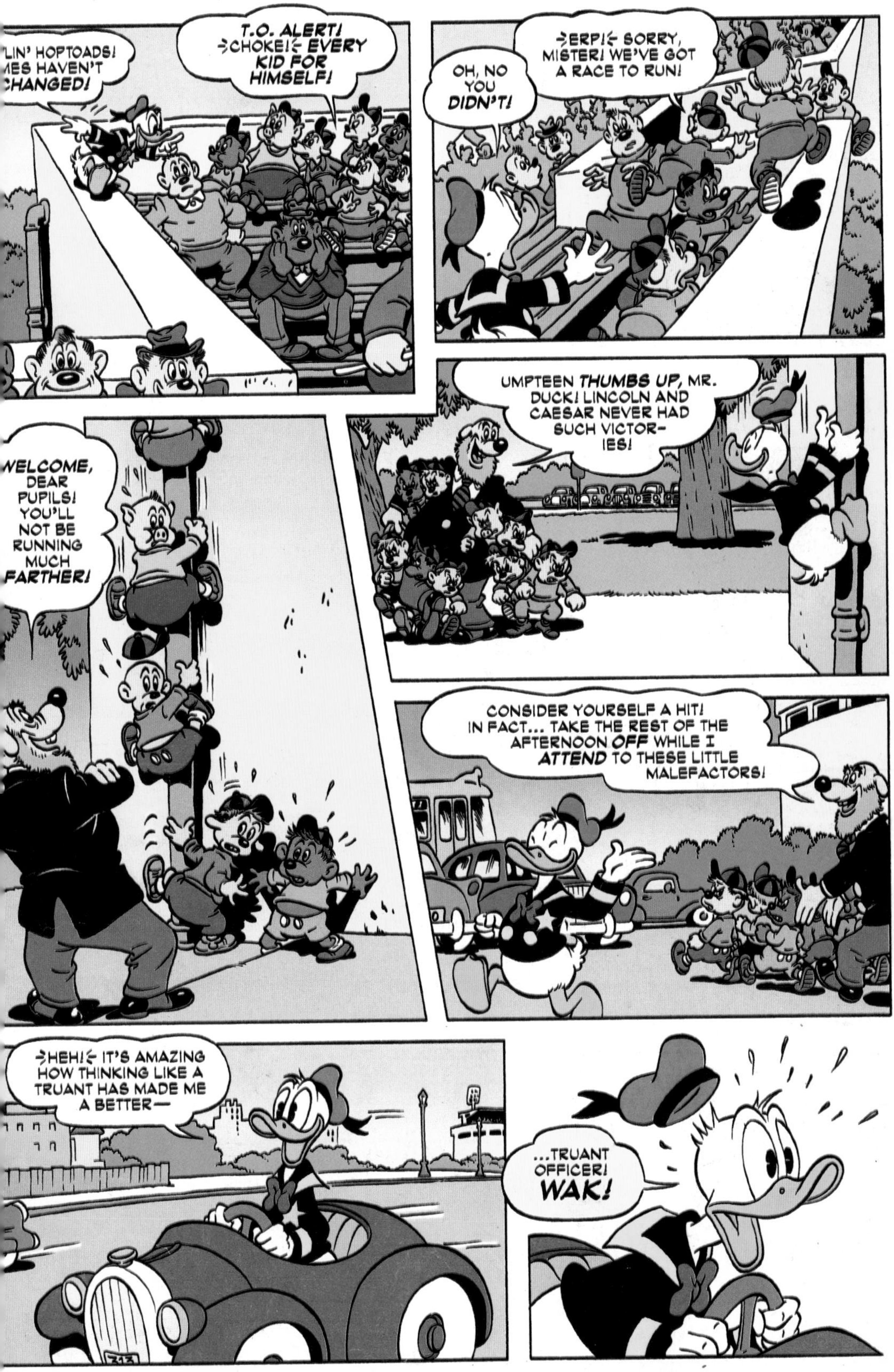

'LIN' HOPTOADS! MES HAVEN'T CHANGED!
T.O. ALERT! ⇢CHOKE!⇠ EVERY KID FOR HIMSELF!
OH, NO YOU DIDN'T!
⇢ERP!⇠ SORRY, MISTER! WE'VE GOT A RACE TO RUN!
WELCOME, DEAR PUPILS! YOU'LL NOT BE RUNNING MUCH FARTHER!
UMPTEEN THUMBS UP, MR. DUCK! LINCOLN AND CAESAR NEVER HAD SUCH VICTOR-IES!
CONSIDER YOURSELF A HIT! IN FACT... TAKE THE REST OF THE AFTERNOON OFF WHILE I ATTEND TO THESE LITTLE MALEFACTORS!
⇢HEH!⇠ IT'S AMAZING HOW THINKING LIKE A TRUANT HAS MADE ME A BETTER—
...TRUANT OFFICER! WAK!

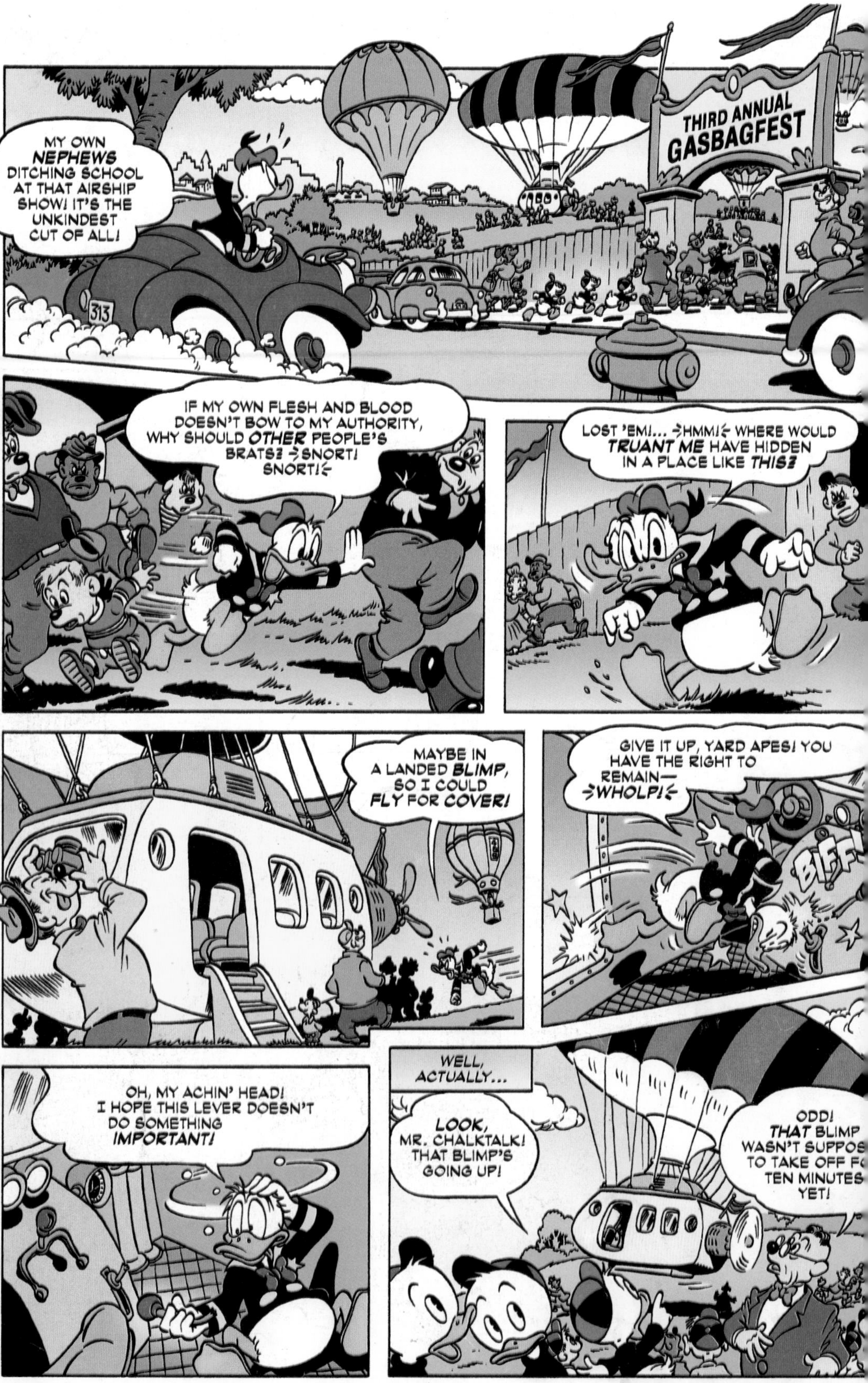
THIRD ANNUAL GASBAGFEST
MY OWN NEPHEWS DITCHING SCHOOL AT THAT AIRSHIP SHOW! IT'S THE UNKINDEST CUT OF ALL!
313
IF MY OWN FLESH AND BLOOD DOESN'T BOW TO MY AUTHORITY, WHY SHOULD OTHER PEOPLE'S BRATS? ⇒SNORT! SNORT!⇐
LOST 'EM!... ⇒HMM!⇐ WHERE WOULD TRUANT ME HAVE HIDDEN IN A PLACE LIKE THIS?
MAYBE IN A LANDED BLIMP, SO I COULD FLY FOR COVER!
GIVE IT UP, YARD APES! YOU HAVE THE RIGHT TO REMAIN— ⇒WHOLP!⇐
BIFF
OH, MY ACHIN' HEAD! I HOPE THIS LEVER DOESN'T DO SOMETHING IMPORTANT!
WELL, ACTUALLY...
LOOK, MR. CHALKTALK! THAT BLIMP'S GOING UP!
ODD! THAT BLIMP WASN'T SUPPOS TO TAKE OFF F TEN MINUTES YET!

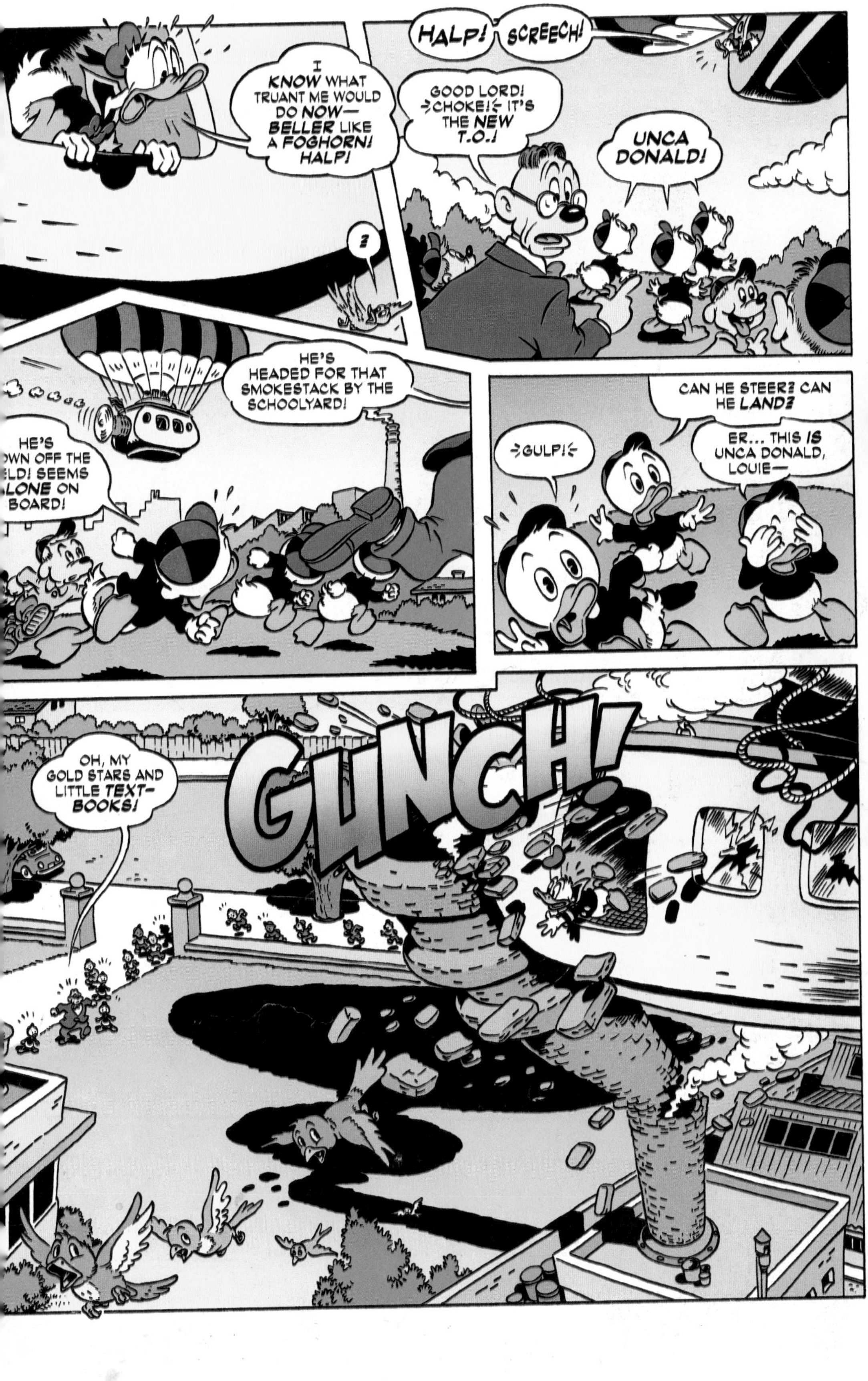
I KNOW WHAT TRUANT ME WOULD DO NOW— BELLER LIKE A FOGHORN! HALP!
?
HALP!
SCREECH!
GOOD LORD! ≠CHOKE!≠ IT'S THE NEW T.O.!
UNCA DONALD!
HE'S HEADED FOR THAT SMOKESTACK BY THE SCHOOLYARD!
HE'S WN OFF THE ELD! SEEMS LONE ON BOARD!
CAN HE STEER? CAN HE LAND?
≠GULP!≠
ER... THIS IS UNCA DONALD, LOUIE—
OH, MY GOLD STARS AND LITTLE TEXT-BOOKS!
GUNCH!

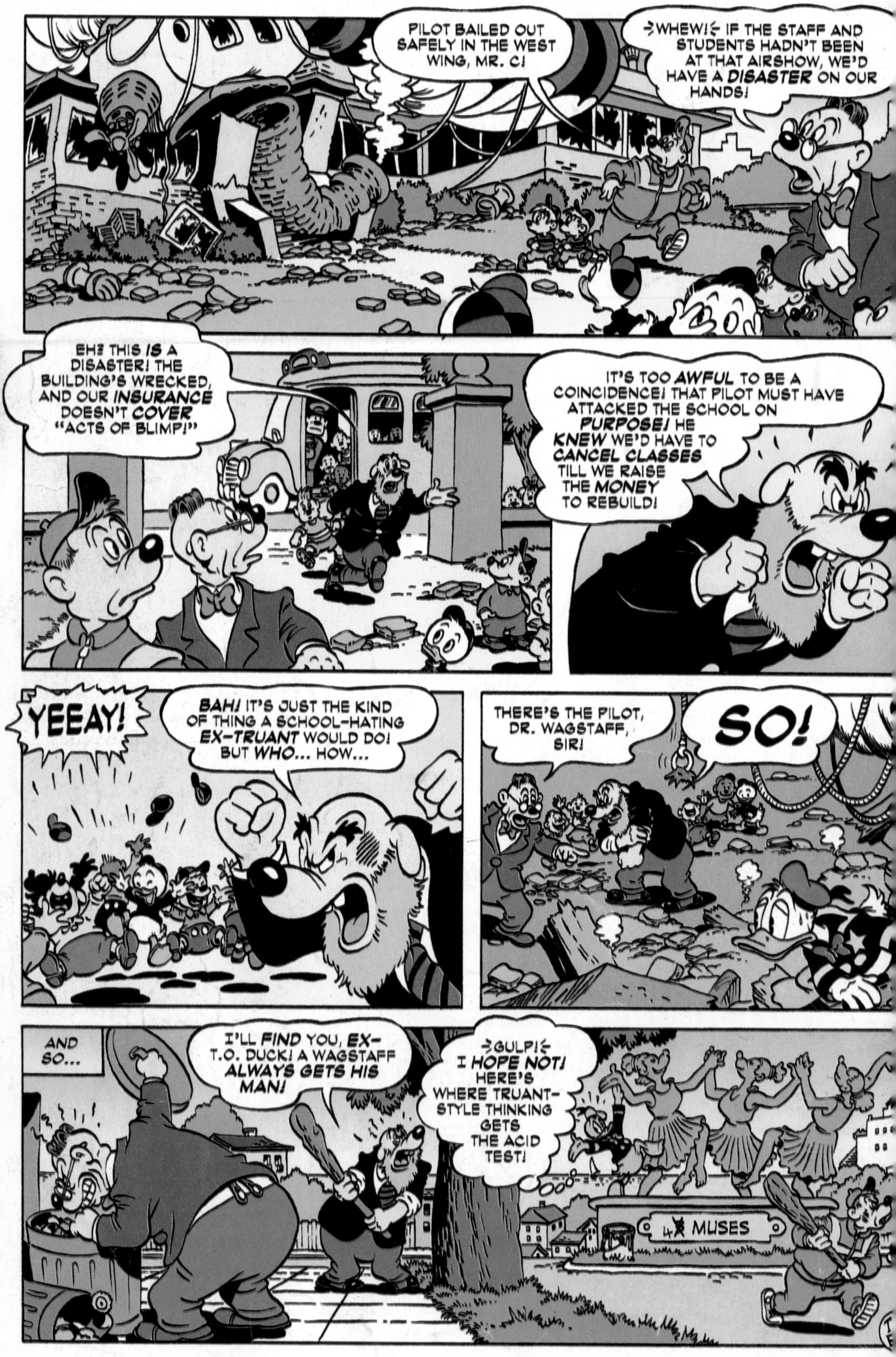
PILOT BAILED OUT SAFELY IN THE WEST WING, MR. C!
WHEW! IF THE STAFF AND STUDENTS HADN'T BEEN AT THAT AIRSHOW, WE'D HAVE A DISASTER ON OUR HANDS!
EH? THIS IS A DISASTER! THE BUILDING'S WRECKED, AND OUR INSURANCE DOESN'T COVER "ACTS OF BLIMP!"
IT'S TOO AWFUL TO BE A COINCIDENCE! THAT PILOT MUST HAVE ATTACKED THE SCHOOL ON PURPOSE! HE KNEW WE'D HAVE TO CANCEL CLASSES TILL WE RAISE THE MONEY TO REBUILD!
YEEAY!
BAH! IT'S JUST THE KIND OF THING A SCHOOL-HATING EX-TRUANT WOULD DO! BUT WHO... HOW...
THERE'S THE PILOT, DR. WAGSTAFF, SIR!
SO!
AND SO...
I'LL FIND YOU, EX-T.O. DUCK! A WAGSTAFF ALWAYS GETS HIS MAN!
GULP! I HOPE NOT! HERE'S WHERE TRUANT-STYLE THINKING GETS THE ACID TEST!
4 MUSES

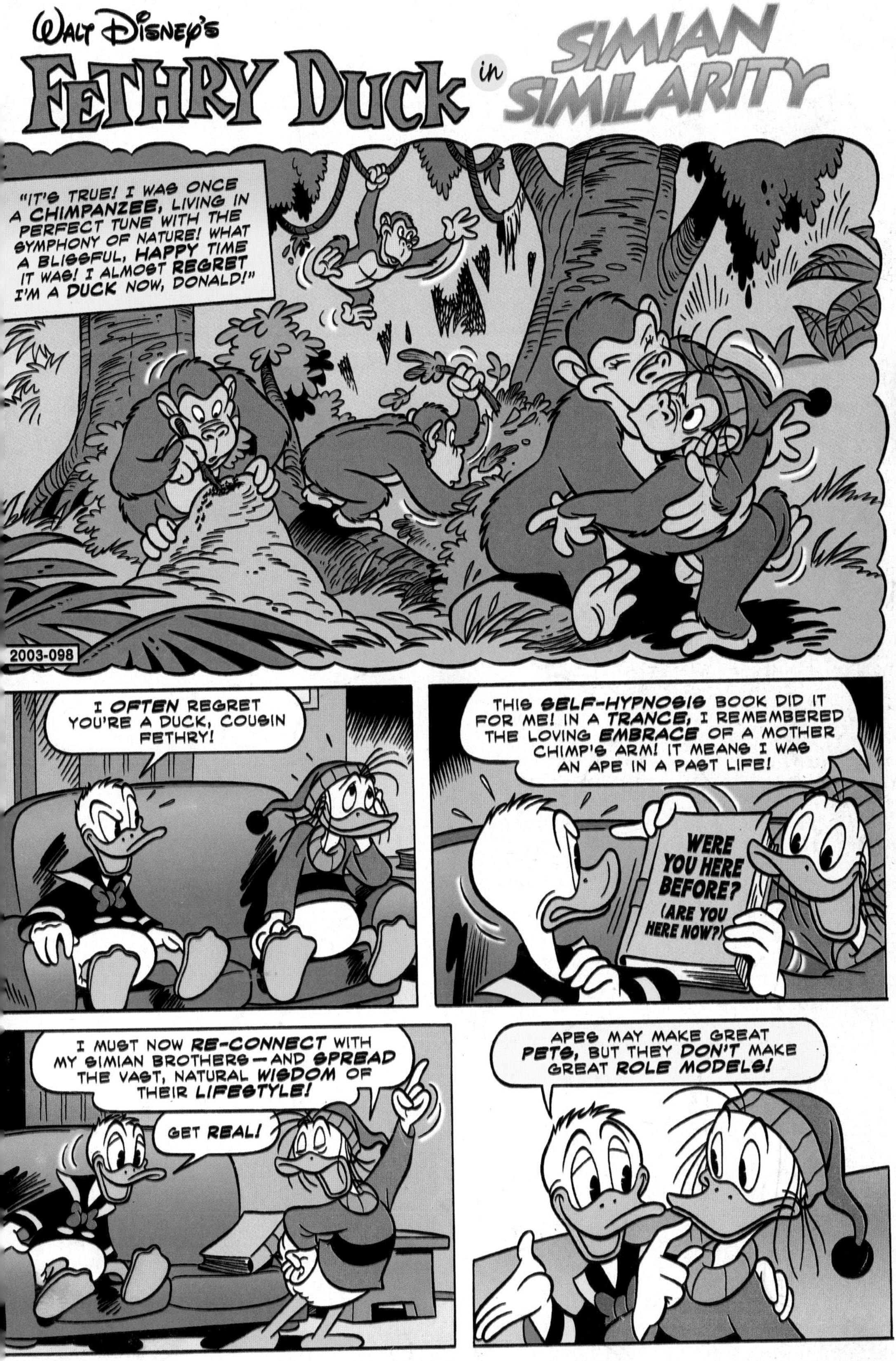

WALT DISNEY'S FETHRY DUCK in SIMIAN SIMILARITY
"IT'S TRUE! I WAS ONCE A CHIMPANZEE, LIVING IN PERFECT TUNE WITH THE SYMPHONY OF NATURE! WHAT A BLISSFUL, HAPPY TIME IT WAS! I ALMOST REGRET I'M A DUCK NOW, DONALD!"
2003-098
I OFTEN REGRET YOU'RE A DUCK, COUSIN FETHRY!
THIS SELF-HYPNOSIS BOOK DID IT FOR ME! IN A TRANCE, I REMEMBERED THE LOVING EMBRACE OF A MOTHER CHIMP'S ARM! IT MEANS I WAS AN APE IN A PAST LIFE!
WERE YOU HERE BEFORE? (ARE YOU HERE NOW?)
I MUST NOW RE-CONNECT WITH MY SIMIAN BROTHERS—AND SPREAD THE VAST, NATURAL WISDOM OF THEIR LIFESTYLE!
GET REAL!
APES MAY MAKE GREAT PETS, BUT THEY DON'T MAKE GREAT ROLE MODELS!

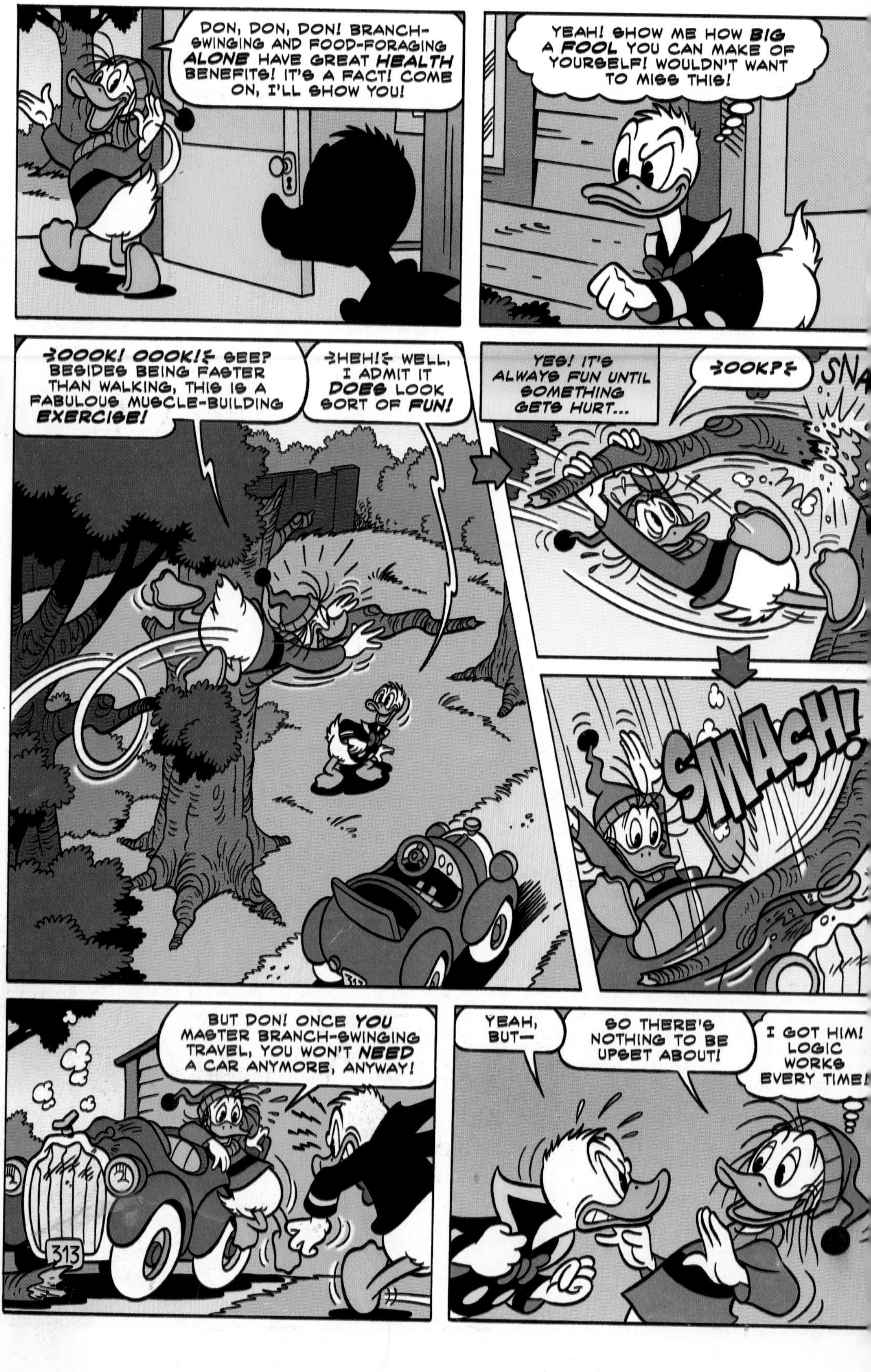
DON, DON, DON! BRANCH-SWINGING AND FOOD-FORAGING ALONE HAVE GREAT HEALTH BENEFITS! IT'S A FACT! COME ON, I'LL SHOW YOU!
YEAH! SHOW ME HOW BIG A FOOL YOU CAN MAKE OF YOURSELF! WOULDN'T WANT TO MISS THIS!
OOOK! OOOK! SEE? BESIDES BEING FASTER THAN WALKING, THIS IS A FABULOUS MUSCLE-BUILDING EXERCISE!
HEH! WELL, I ADMIT IT DOES LOOK SORT OF FUN!
YES! IT'S ALWAYS FUN UNTIL SOMETHING GETS HURT...
OOK?
SMASH!
313
BUT DON! ONCE YOU MASTER BRANCH-SWINGING TRAVEL, YOU WON'T NEED A CAR ANYMORE, ANYWAY!
YEAH, BUT—
SO THERE'S NOTHING TO BE UPSET ABOUT!
I GOT HIM! LOGIC WORKS EVERY TIME!

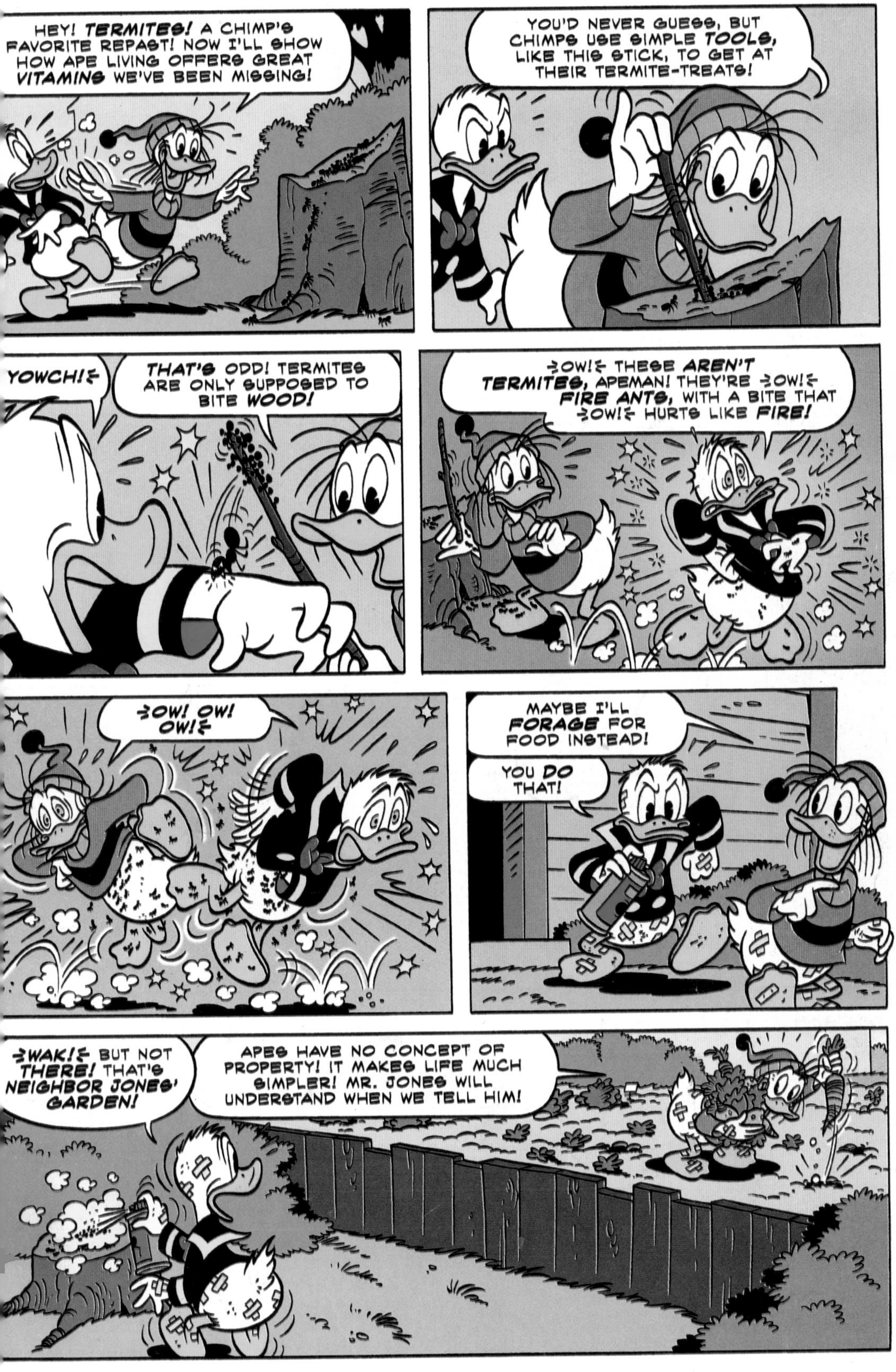
HEY! TERMITES! A CHIMP'S FAVORITE REPAST! NOW I'LL SHOW HOW APE LIVING OFFERS GREAT VITAMINS WE'VE BEEN MISSING!
YOU'D NEVER GUESS, BUT CHIMPS USE SIMPLE TOOLS, LIKE THIS STICK, TO GET AT THEIR TERMITE-TREATS!
YOWCH!
THAT'S ODD! TERMITES ARE ONLY SUPPOSED TO BITE WOOD!
OW! THESE AREN'T TERMITES, APEMAN! THEY'RE OW! FIRE ANTS, WITH A BITE THAT OW! HURTS LIKE FIRE!
OW! OW! OW!
MAYBE I'LL FORAGE FOR FOOD INSTEAD!
YOU DO THAT!
WAK! BUT NOT THERE! THAT'S NEIGHBOR JONES' GARDEN!
APES HAVE NO CONCEPT OF PROPERTY! IT MAKES LIFE MUCH SIMPLER! MR. JONES WILL UNDERSTAND WHEN WE TELL HIM!

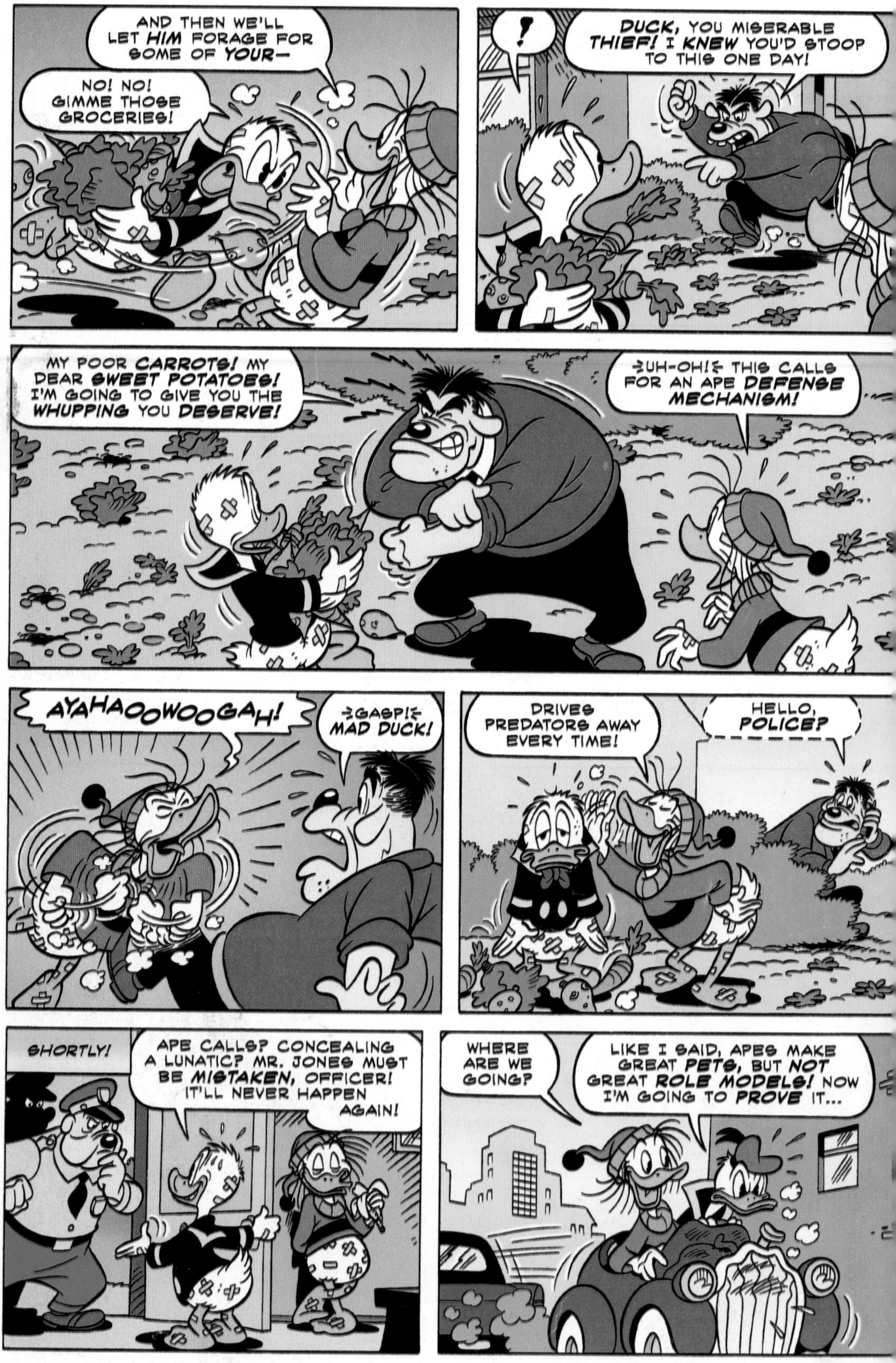
AND THEN WE'LL LET HIM FORAGE FOR SOME OF YOUR—
NO! NO! GIMME THOSE GROCERIES!
!
DUCK, YOU MISERABLE THIEF! I KNEW YOU'D STOOP TO THIS ONE DAY!
MY POOR CARROTS! MY DEAR SWEET POTATOES! I'M GOING TO GIVE YOU THE WHUPPING YOU DESERVE!
UH-OH! THIS CALLS FOR AN APE DEFENSE MECHANISM!
AYAHAOOWOOGAH!
GASP! MAD DUCK!
DRIVES PREDATORS AWAY EVERY TIME!
HELLO, POLICE?
SHORTLY!
APE CALLS? CONCEALING A LUNATIC? MR. JONES MUST BE MISTAKEN, OFFICER! IT'LL NEVER HAPPEN AGAIN!
WHERE ARE WE GOING?
LIKE I SAID, APES MAKE GREAT PETS, BUT NOT GREAT ROLE MODELS! NOW I'M GOING TO PROVE IT...

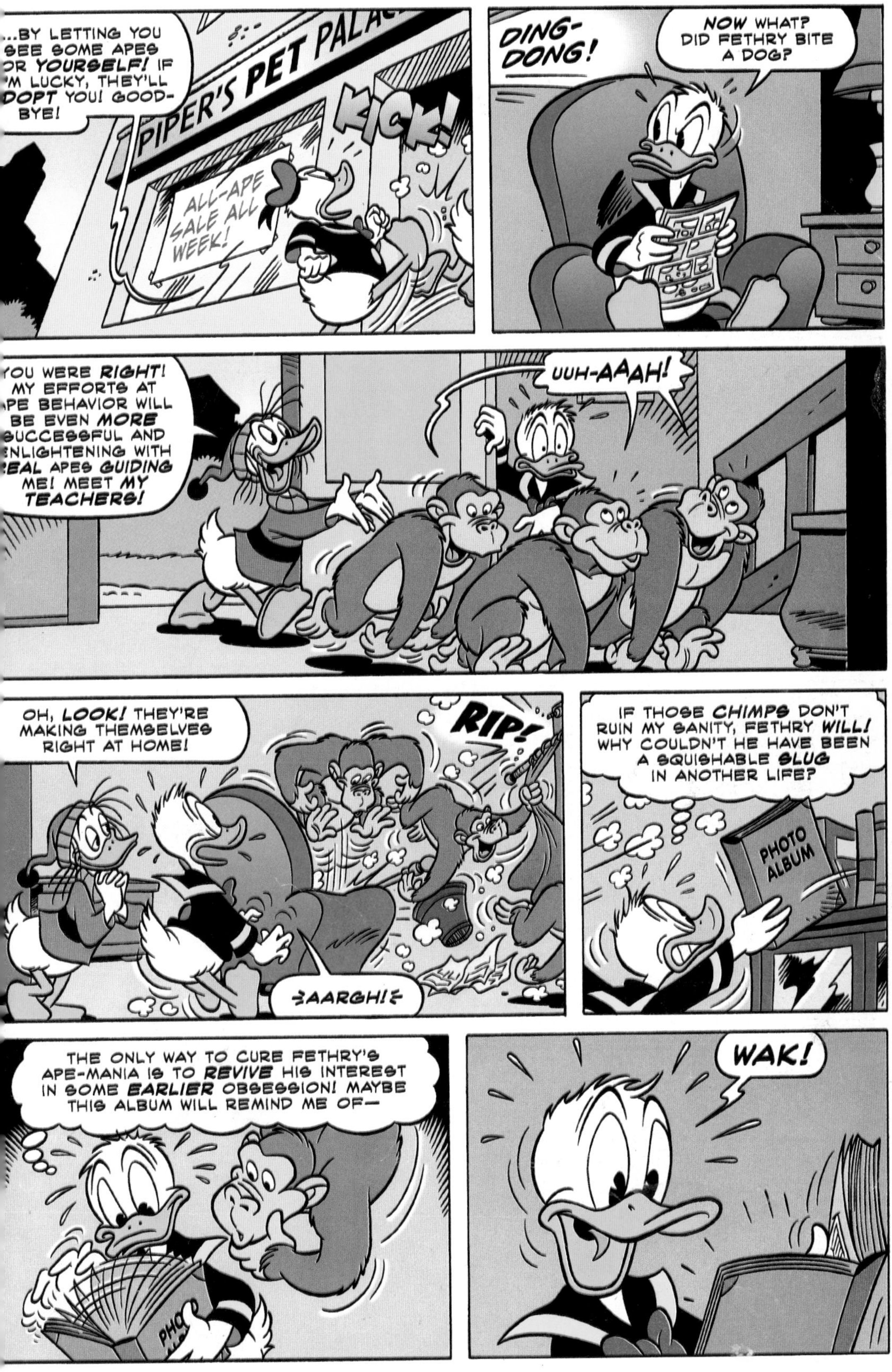

...BY LETTING YOU SEE SOME APES OR YOURSELF! IF 'M LUCKY, THEY'LL DOPT YOU! GOOD-BYE!
PIPER'S PET PALA
ALL-APE SALE ALL WEEK!
KICK!
DING-DONG!
NOW WHAT? DID FETHRY BITE A DOG?
YOU WERE RIGHT! MY EFFORTS AT APE BEHAVIOR WILL BE EVEN MORE SUCCESSFUL AND ENLIGHTENING WITH REAL APES GUIDING ME! MEET MY TEACHERS!
UUH-AAAH!
OH, LOOK! THEY'RE MAKING THEMSELVES RIGHT AT HOME!
RIP!
AARGH!
IF THOSE CHIMPS DON'T RUIN MY SANITY, FETHRY WILL! WHY COULDN'T HE HAVE BEEN A SQUISHABLE SLUG IN ANOTHER LIFE?
PHOTO ALBUM
THE ONLY WAY TO CURE FETHRY'S APE-MANIA IS TO REVIVE HIS INTEREST IN SOME EARLIER OBSESSION! MAYBE THIS ALBUM WILL REMIND ME OF—
WAK!

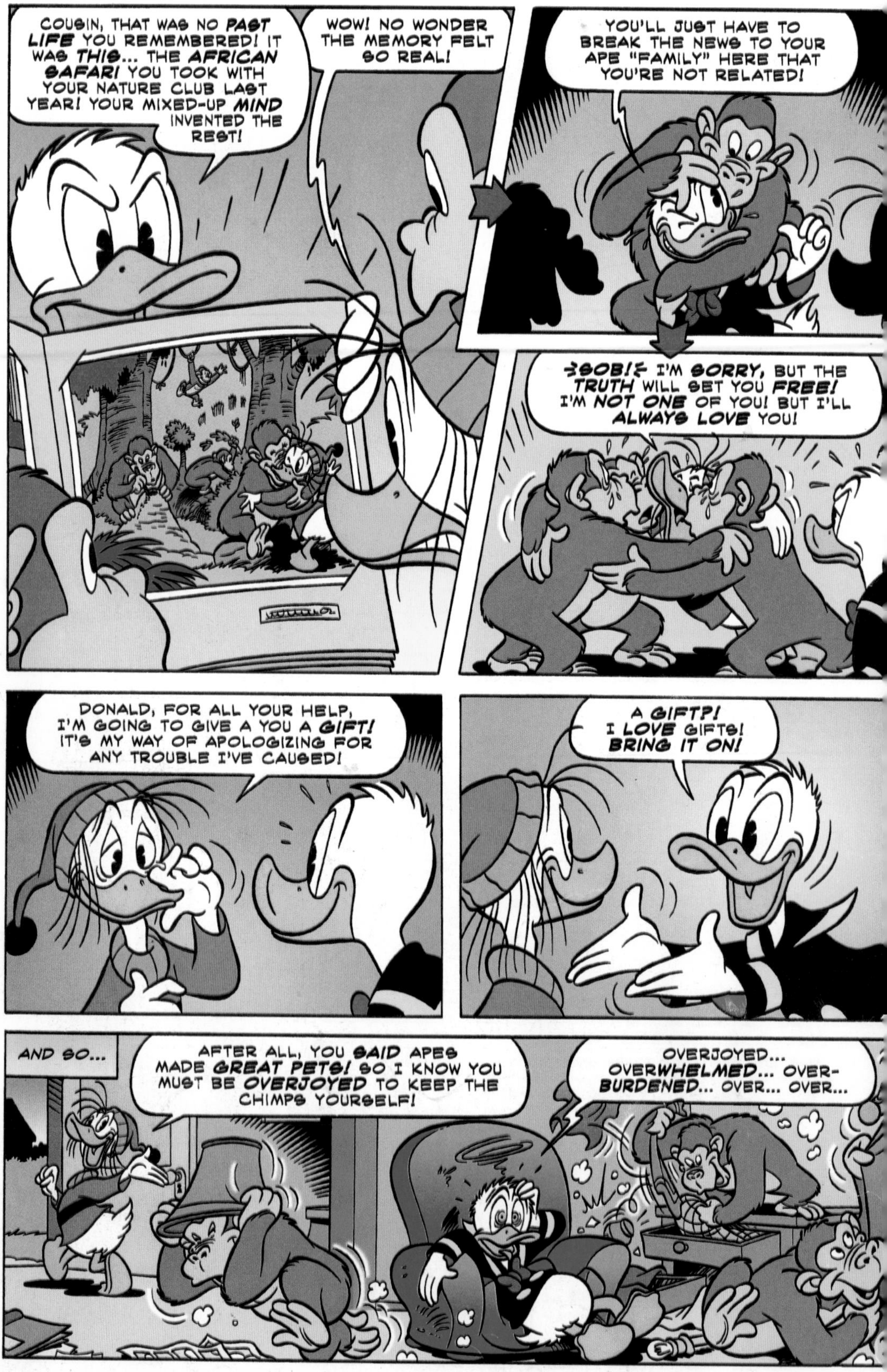
COUSIN, THAT WAS NO PAST LIFE YOU REMEMBERED! IT WAS THIS... THE AFRICAN SAFARI YOU TOOK WITH YOUR NATURE CLUB LAST YEAR! YOUR MIXED-UP MIND INVENTED THE REST!
WOW! NO WONDER THE MEMORY FELT SO REAL!
YOU'LL JUST HAVE TO BREAK THE NEWS TO YOUR APE "FAMILY" HERE THAT YOU'RE NOT RELATED!
SOB! I'M SORRY, BUT THE TRUTH WILL SET YOU FREE! I'M NOT ONE OF YOU! BUT I'LL ALWAYS LOVE YOU!
DONALD, FOR ALL YOUR HELP, I'M GOING TO GIVE A YOU A GIFT! IT'S MY WAY OF APOLOGIZING FOR ANY TROUBLE I'VE CAUSED!
A GIFT?! I LOVE GIFTS! BRING IT ON!
AND SO...
AFTER ALL, YOU SAID APES MADE GREAT PETS! SO I KNOW YOU MUST BE OVERJOYED TO KEEP THE CHIMPS YOURSELF!
OVERJOYED... OVERWHELMED... OVER-BURDENED... OVER... OVER...

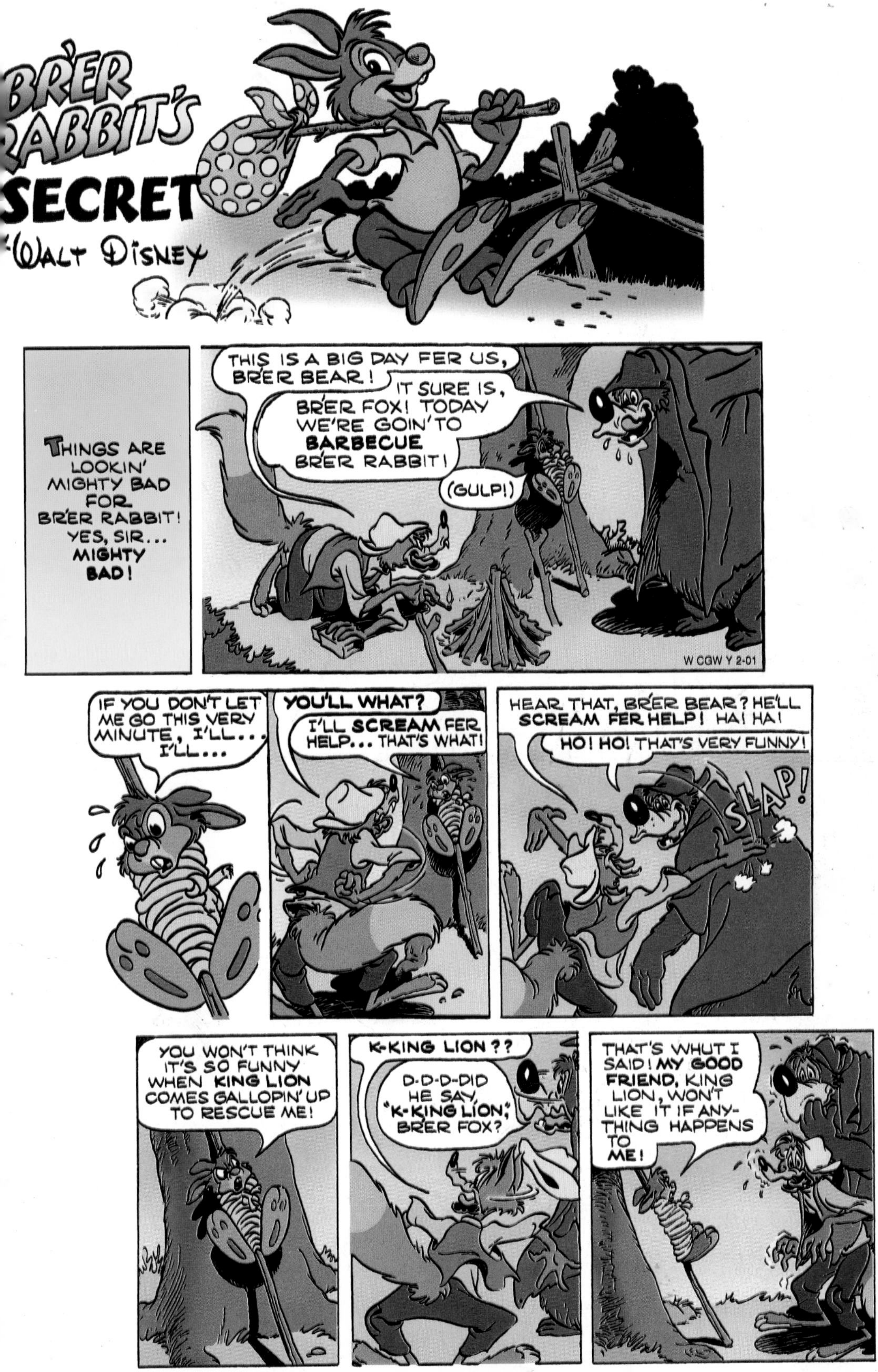
BR'ER RABBIT'S SECRET
WALT DISNEY
THINGS ARE LOOKIN' MIGHTY BAD FOR BR'ER RABBIT! YES, SIR... MIGHTY BAD!
THIS IS A BIG DAY FER US, BR'ER BEAR!
IT SURE IS, BR'ER FOX! TODAY WE'RE GOIN' TO BARBECUE BR'ER RABBIT!
(GULP!)
W CGW Y 2-01
IF YOU DON'T LET ME GO THIS VERY MINUTE, I'LL... I'LL...
YOU'LL WHAT?
I'LL SCREAM FER HELP... THAT'S WHAT!
HEAR THAT, BR'ER BEAR? HE'LL SCREAM FER HELP! HA! HA!
HO! HO! THAT'S VERY FUNNY!
SLAP!
YOU WON'T THINK IT'S SO FUNNY WHEN KING LION COMES GALLOPIN' UP TO RESCUE ME!
K-KING LION??
D-D-D-DID HE SAY, "K-KING LION," BR'ER FOX?
THAT'S WHUT I SAID! MY GOOD FRIEND, KING LION, WON'T LIKE IT IF ANY-THING HAPPENS TO ME!

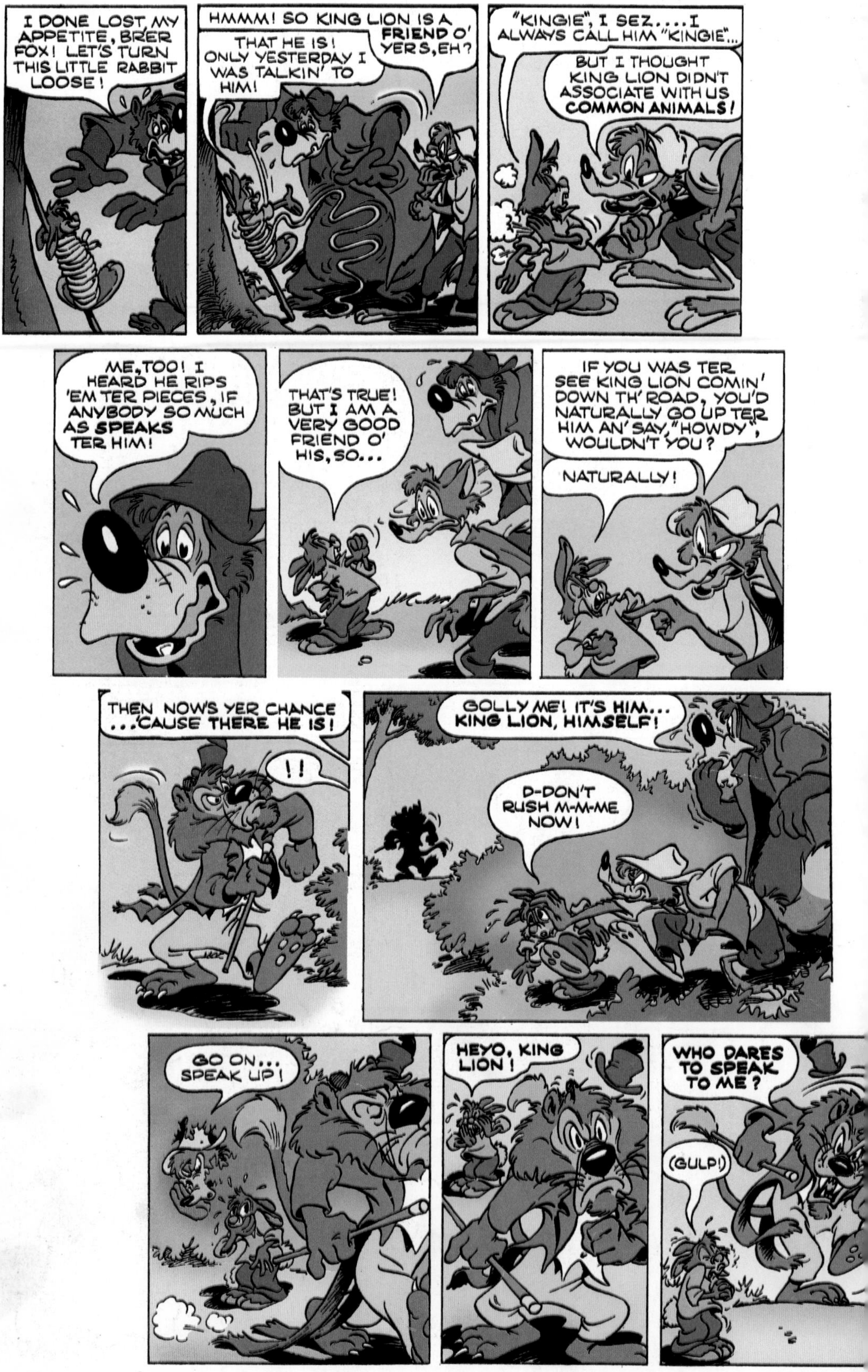
I DONE LOST MY APPETITE, BRER FOX! LET'S TURN THIS LITTLE RABBIT LOOSE!
HMMM! SO KING LION IS A FRIEND O' YERS, EH?
THAT HE IS! ONLY YESTERDAY I WAS TALKIN' TO HIM!
"KINGIE", I SEZ....I ALWAYS CALL HIM "KINGIE"...
BUT I THOUGHT KING LION DIDN'T ASSOCIATE WITH US COMMON ANIMALS!
ME, TOO! I HEARD HE RIPS 'EM TER PIECES, IF ANYBODY SO MUCH AS SPEAKS TER HIM!
THAT'S TRUE! BUT I AM A VERY GOOD FRIEND O' HIS, SO...
IF YOU WAS TER SEE KING LION COMIN' DOWN TH' ROAD, YOU'D NATURALLY GO UP TER HIM AN' SAY, "HOWDY", WOULDN'T YOU?
NATURALLY!
THEN NOW'S YER CHANCE ...'CAUSE THERE HE IS!
!!
GOLLY ME! IT'S HIM... KING LION, HIMSELF!
D-DON'T RUSH M-M-ME NOW!
GO ON... SPEAK UP!
HEYO, KING LION!
WHO DARES TO SPEAK TO ME?
(GULP!)

ABBIT! COME HERE!

Y-Y-YES, SIR!

TEE HEE!

BR'ER RABBIT WAS SPOOFIN' US! HE AIN'T FRIENDS WITH KING LION!

WHEN KING LION GITS THROUGH WITH HIM, WE'LL PICK UP TH' PIECES AN' HAVE US SOME RABBIT STEW!

SO THAT'S WHY YOU SPOKE TO ME?

YES, SIR, YER HONOR! I WANTED TER KNOW IF YOU'D ACCEPT A GIFT FROM ME O' SOME WILD DUCKS AN' SOME WILD TURKEYS!

THEN HE REALLY IS FRIENDLY WITH KING LION!

LOOKS THAT WAY, BR'ER BEAR!

SEE YOU TOMORROW THEN, BR'ER RABBIT!

YES, SIR, YER HONOR!

WHEW! I GOT OUT O' THAT... BUT WHERE AM I GONNA GIT THOSE BIRDS I PROMISED HIM?

IF I DON'T GIT 'EM NOW, HE'S GONNA BE POWERFUL MAD AT ME.... AN' ME WITHOUT A SHOOTIN' IRON TO HUNT 'EM WITH!

BR'ER RABBIT, OL' FRIEND! WAIT FER ME!

WAIT FER ME, TOO!

BR'ER FOX AN' BR'ER BEAR.... THEY BOTH HAVE SHOOTIN' IRONS!

TELL US, BR'ER RABBIT... HOW'D YOU GIT SO FRIENDLY WITH KING LION?

YEAH... TELL US!

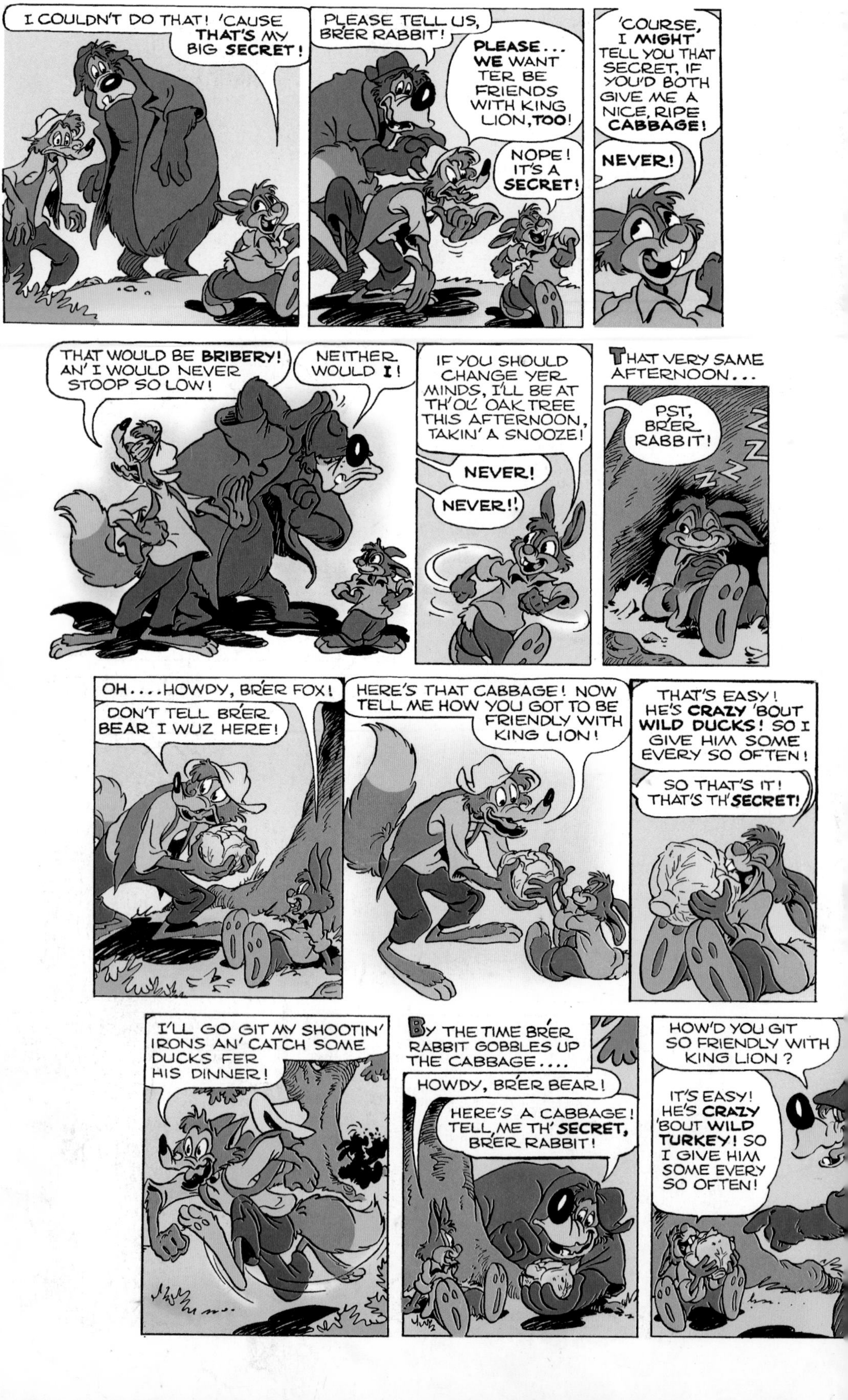
I COULDN'T DO THAT! 'CAUSE THAT'S MY BIG SECRET!
PLEASE TELL US, BR'ER RABBIT!
PLEASE... WE WANT TER BE FRIENDS WITH KING LION, TOO!
NOPE! IT'S A SECRET!
'COURSE, I MIGHT TELL YOU THAT SECRET, IF YOU'D BOTH GIVE ME A NICE, RIPE CABBAGE!
NEVER!
THAT WOULD BE BRIBERY! AN' I WOULD NEVER STOOP SO LOW!
NEITHER WOULD I!
IF YOU SHOULD CHANGE YER MINDS, I'LL BE AT TH' OL' OAK TREE THIS AFTERNOON, TAKIN' A SNOOZE!
NEVER!
NEVER!!
THAT VERY SAME AFTERNOON...
PST, BR'ER RABBIT!
OH....HOWDY, BR'ER FOX!
DON'T TELL BR'ER BEAR I WUZ HERE!
HERE'S THAT CABBAGE! NOW TELL ME HOW YOU GOT TO BE FRIENDLY WITH KING LION!
THAT'S EASY! HE'S CRAZY 'BOUT WILD DUCKS! SO I GIVE HIM SOME EVERY SO OFTEN!
SO THAT'S IT! THAT'S TH' SECRET!
I'LL GO GIT MY SHOOTIN' IRONS AN' CATCH SOME DUCKS FER HIS DINNER!
BY THE TIME BR'ER RABBIT GOBBLES UP THE CABBAGE....
HOWDY, BR'ER BEAR!
HERE'S A CABBAGE! TELL ME TH' SECRET, BR'ER RABBIT!
HOW'D YOU GIT SO FRIENDLY WITH KING LION?
IT'S EASY! HE'S CRAZY 'BOUT WILD TURKEY! SO I GIVE HIM SOME EVERY SO OFTEN!

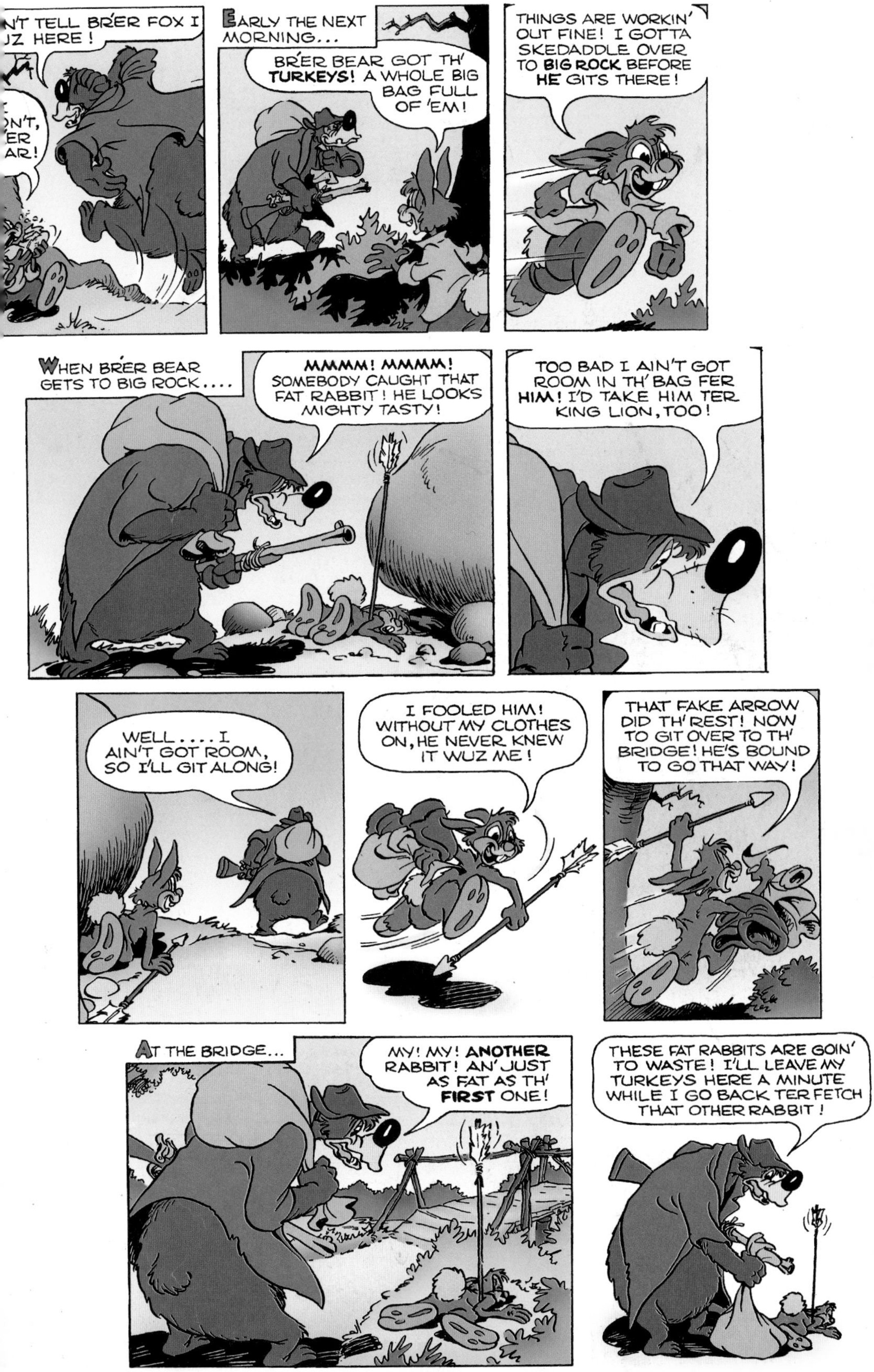

N'T TELL BR'ER FOX I
UZ HERE!
N'T,
ER
AR!
EARLY THE NEXT MORNING...
BR'ER BEAR GOT TH' TURKEYS! A WHOLE BIG BAG FULL OF 'EM!
THINGS ARE WORKIN' OUT FINE! I GOTTA SKEDADDLE OVER TO BIG ROCK BEFORE HE GITS THERE!
WHEN BR'ER BEAR GETS TO BIG ROCK....
MMMM! MMMM! SOMEBODY CAUGHT THAT FAT RABBIT! HE LOOKS MIGHTY TASTY!
TOO BAD I AIN'T GOT ROOM IN TH' BAG FER HIM! I'D TAKE HIM TER KING LION, TOO!
WELL.... I AIN'T GOT ROOM, SO I'LL GIT ALONG!
I FOOLED HIM! WITHOUT MY CLOTHES ON, HE NEVER KNEW IT WUZ ME!
THAT FAKE ARROW DID TH' REST! NOW TO GIT OVER TO TH' BRIDGE! HE'S BOUND TO GO THAT WAY!
AT THE BRIDGE...
MY! MY! ANOTHER RABBIT! AN' JUST AS FAT AS TH' FIRST ONE!
THESE FAT RABBITS ARE GOIN' TO WASTE! I'LL LEAVE MY TURKEYS HERE A MINUTE WHILE I GO BACK TER FETCH THAT OTHER RABBIT!

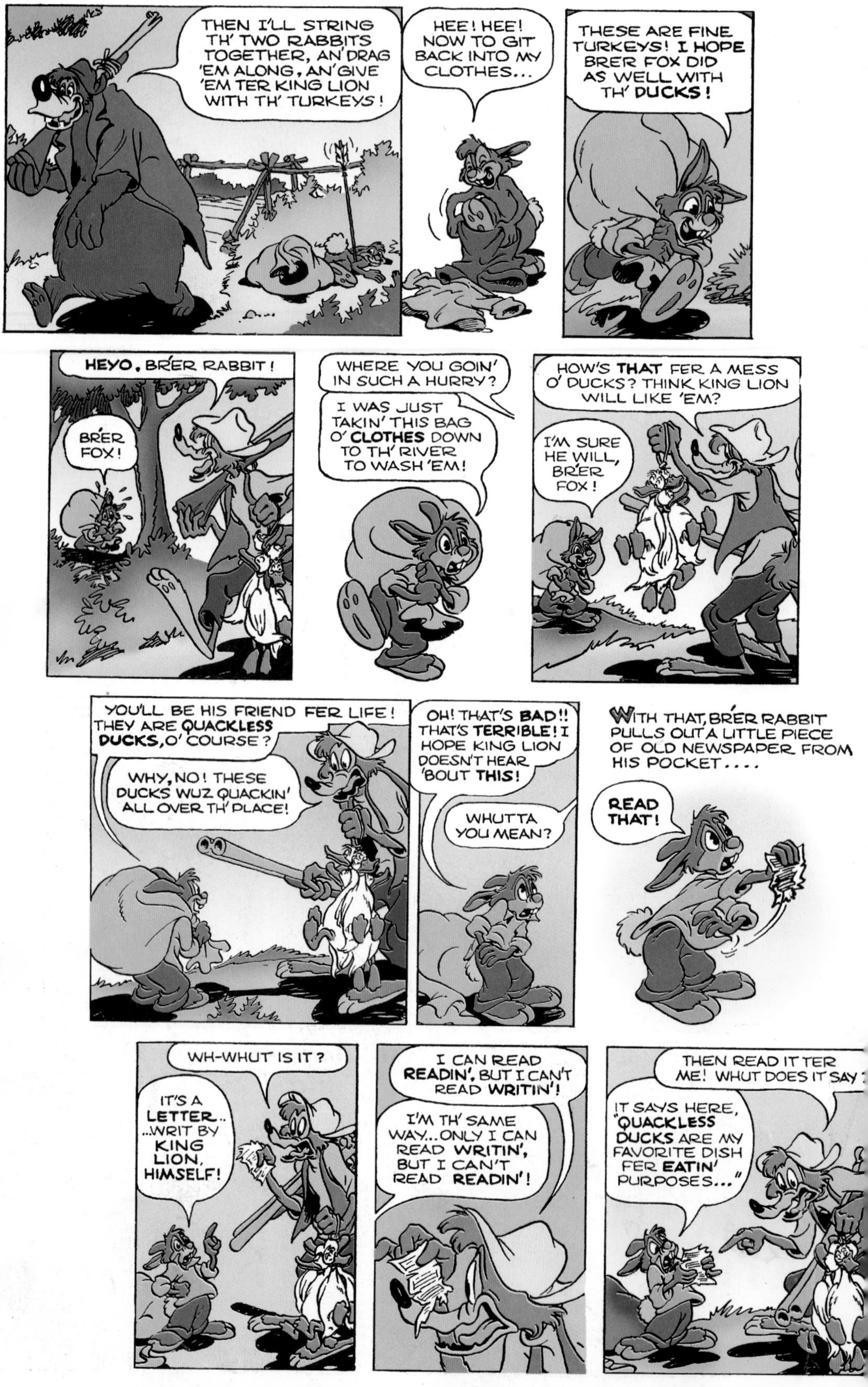
THEN I'LL STRING TH' TWO RABBITS TOGETHER, AN' DRAG 'EM ALONG, AN' GIVE 'EM TER KING LION WITH TH' TURKEYS!
HEE! HEE! NOW TO GIT BACK INTO MY CLOTHES...
THESE ARE FINE TURKEYS! I HOPE BRER FOX DID AS WELL WITH TH' DUCKS!
HEYO, BR'ER RABBIT!
BR'ER FOX!
WHERE YOU GOIN' IN SUCH A HURRY?
I WAS JUST TAKIN' THIS BAG O' CLOTHES DOWN TO TH' RIVER TO WASH 'EM!
HOW'S THAT FER A MESS O' DUCKS? THINK KING LION WILL LIKE 'EM?
I'M SURE HE WILL, BR'ER FOX!
YOU'LL BE HIS FRIEND FER LIFE! THEY ARE QUACKLESS DUCKS, O' COURSE?
WHY, NO! THESE DUCKS WUZ QUACKIN' ALL OVER TH' PLACE!
OH! THAT'S BAD!! THAT'S TERRIBLE! I HOPE KING LION DOESN'T HEAR 'BOUT THIS!
WHUTTA YOU MEAN?
WITH THAT, BR'ER RABBIT PULLS OUT A LITTLE PIECE OF OLD NEWSPAPER FROM HIS POCKET....
READ THAT!
WH-WHUT IS IT?
IT'S A LETTER.. ..WRIT BY KING LION, HIMSELF!
I CAN READ READIN', BUT I CAN'T READ WRITIN'!
I'M TH' SAME WAY... ONLY I CAN READ WRITIN', BUT I CAN'T READ READIN'!
THEN READ IT TER ME! WHUT DOES IT SAY?
IT SAYS HERE, "QUACKLESS DUCKS ARE MY FAVORITE DISH FER EATIN' PURPOSES..."

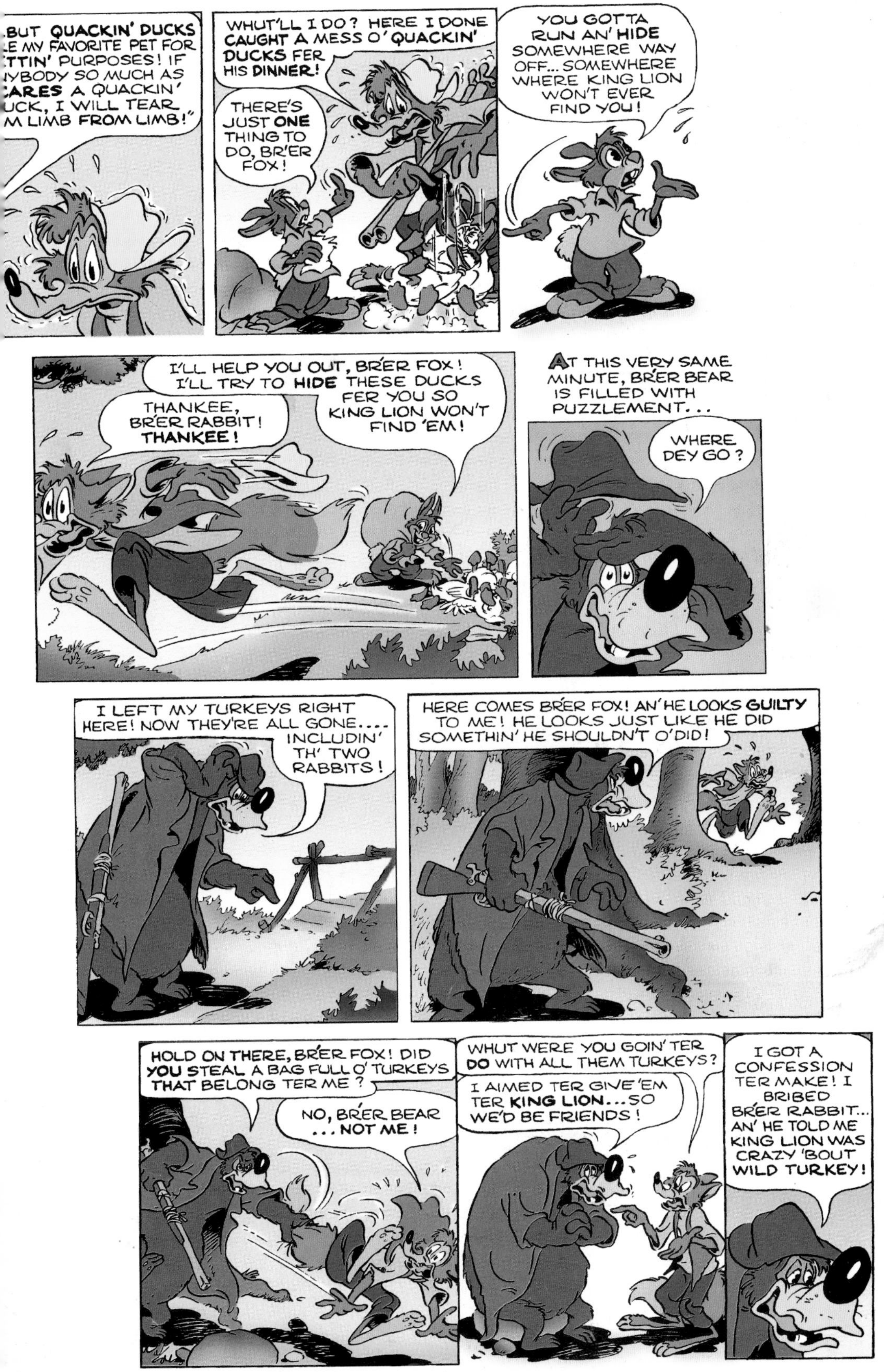
...BUT QUACKIN' DUCKS ...E MY FAVORITE PET FOR ...TTIN' PURPOSES! IF ...NYBODY SO MUCH AS ...CARES A QUACKIN' ...UCK, I WILL TEAR ...M LIMB FROM LIMB!"
WHUT'LL I DO? HERE I DONE CAUGHT A MESS O' QUACKIN' DUCKS FER HIS DINNER!
THERE'S JUST ONE THING TO DO, BR'ER FOX!
YOU GOTTA RUN AN' HIDE SOMEWHERE WAY OFF... SOMEWHERE WHERE KING LION WON'T EVER FIND YOU!
I'LL HELP YOU OUT, BR'ER FOX! I'LL TRY TO HIDE THESE DUCKS FER YOU SO KING LION WON'T FIND 'EM!
THANKEE, BR'ER RABBIT! THANKEE!
AT THIS VERY SAME MINUTE, BR'ER BEAR IS FILLED WITH PUZZLEMENT...
WHERE DEY GO?
I LEFT MY TURKEYS RIGHT HERE! NOW THEY'RE ALL GONE.... INCLUDIN' TH' TWO RABBITS!
HERE COMES BR'ER FOX! AN' HE LOOKS GUILTY TO ME! HE LOOKS JUST LIKE HE DID SOMETHIN' HE SHOULDN'T O'DID!
HOLD ON THERE, BR'ER FOX! DID YOU STEAL A BAG FULL O' TURKEYS THAT BELONG TER ME?
NO, BR'ER BEAR ... NOT ME!
WHUT WERE YOU GOIN' TER DO WITH ALL THEM TURKEYS?
I AIMED TER GIVE 'EM TER KING LION... SO WE'D BE FRIENDS!
I GOT A CONFESSION TER MAKE! I BRIBED BR'ER RABBIT... AN' HE TOLD ME KING LION WAS CRAZY 'BOUT WILD TURKEY!

THAT'S FUNNY! HE TOLD ME THAT IT WUZ DUCKS HE LIKED.... TH' QUACKLESS KIND!
SURE ENUFF?
OH! OH! OHHHHH! I SEE IT ALL NOW! THAT NO-GOOD RABBIT HAS TRICKED US AG'IN, BR'ER BEAR!
I BET THAT BAG WASN'T FILLED WITH CLOTHES, AT ALL!
HE WENT THIS WAY! THERE'S HIS FOOTPRINTS!
THAT DIRTY, LOW-DOWN...
JUST WAIT'LL I GIT MY PAWS ON THAT RABBIT!
SHHHH, BR'ER FOX!
I HEAR VOICES ON TH' OTHER SIDE O' TH' BUSHES!
IT'S MY WILD TURKEYS!
AN' MY WILD DUCKS.... TH' QUACKIN' KIND!
THANKEE, BR'ER RABBIT! AND REMEMBER.... IF YOU EVER NEED HELP, JUST CALL FOR ME!
I'LL REMEMBER THAT, KING LION, OL' FRIEND! YES, SIR, I'LL SURE REMEMBER THAT! HEE! HEE!
The End

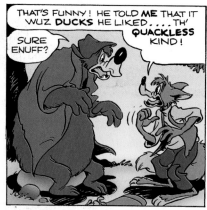

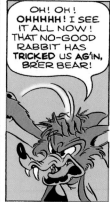

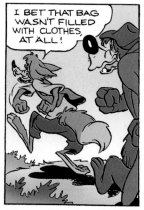

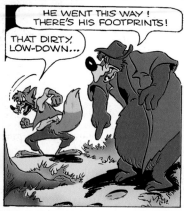

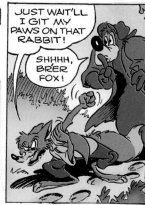

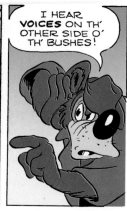

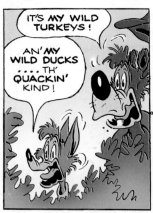

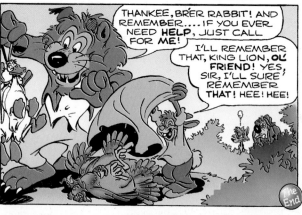

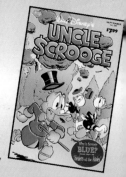

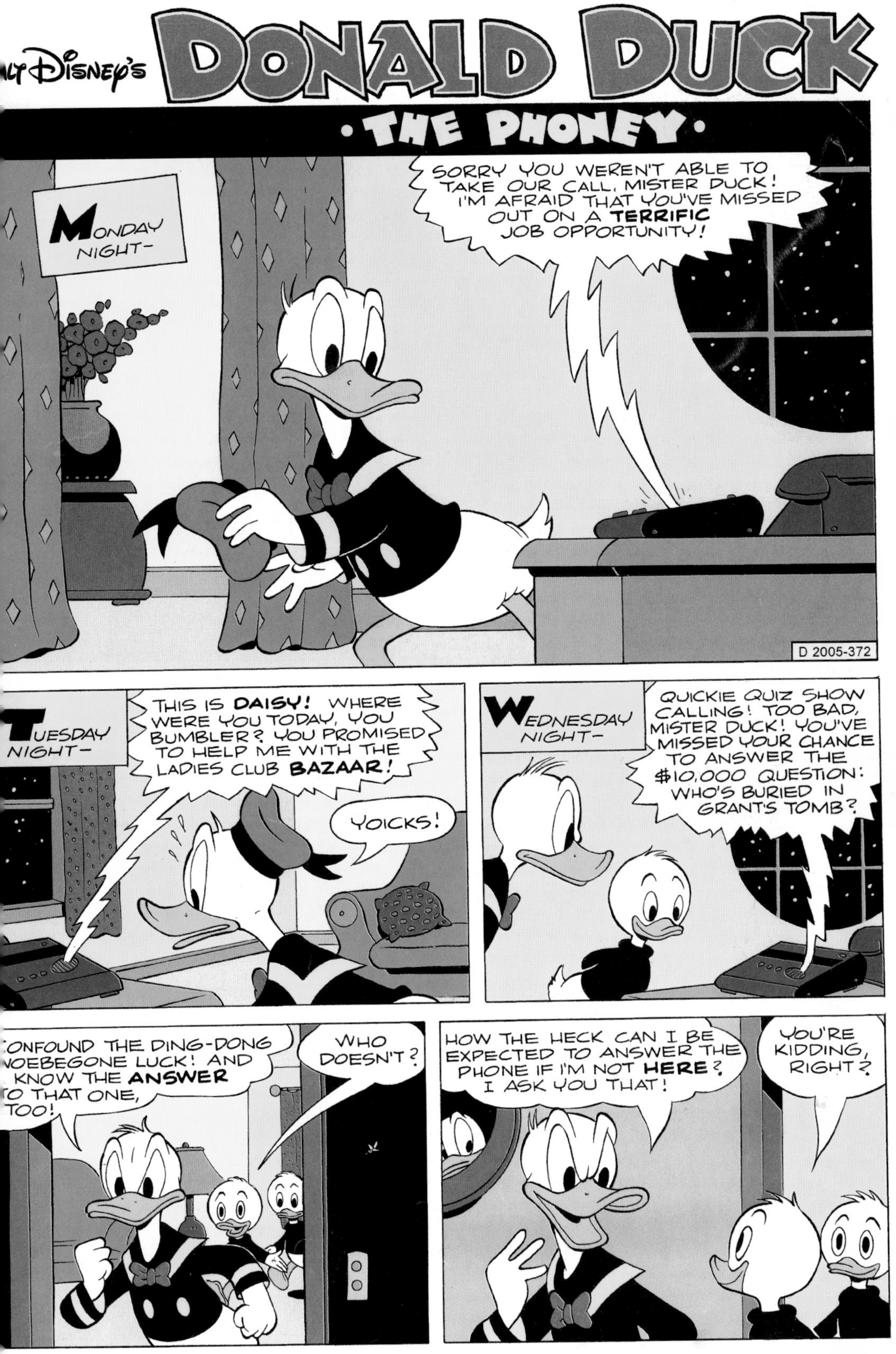

WALT DISNEY'S DONALD DUCK
· THE PHONEY ·
MONDAY NIGHT-
SORRY YOU WEREN'T ABLE TO TAKE OUR CALL, MISTER DUCK! I'M AFRAID THAT YOU'VE MISSED OUT ON A TERRIFIC JOB OPPORTUNITY!
D 2005-372
TUESDAY NIGHT-
THIS IS DAISY! WHERE WERE YOU TODAY, YOU BUMBLER? YOU PROMISED TO HELP ME WITH THE LADIES CLUB BAZAAR!
YOICKS!
WEDNESDAY NIGHT-
QUICKIE QUIZ SHOW CALLING! TOO BAD, MISTER DUCK! YOU'VE MISSED YOUR CHANCE TO ANSWER THE $10,000 QUESTION: WHO'S BURIED IN GRANT'S TOMB?
CONFOUND THE DING-DONG WOEBEGONE LUCK! AND I KNOW THE ANSWER TO THAT ONE, TOO!
WHO DOESN'T?
HOW THE HECK CAN I BE EXPECTED TO ANSWER THE PHONE IF I'M NOT HERE? I ASK YOU THAT!
YOU'RE KIDDING, RIGHT?

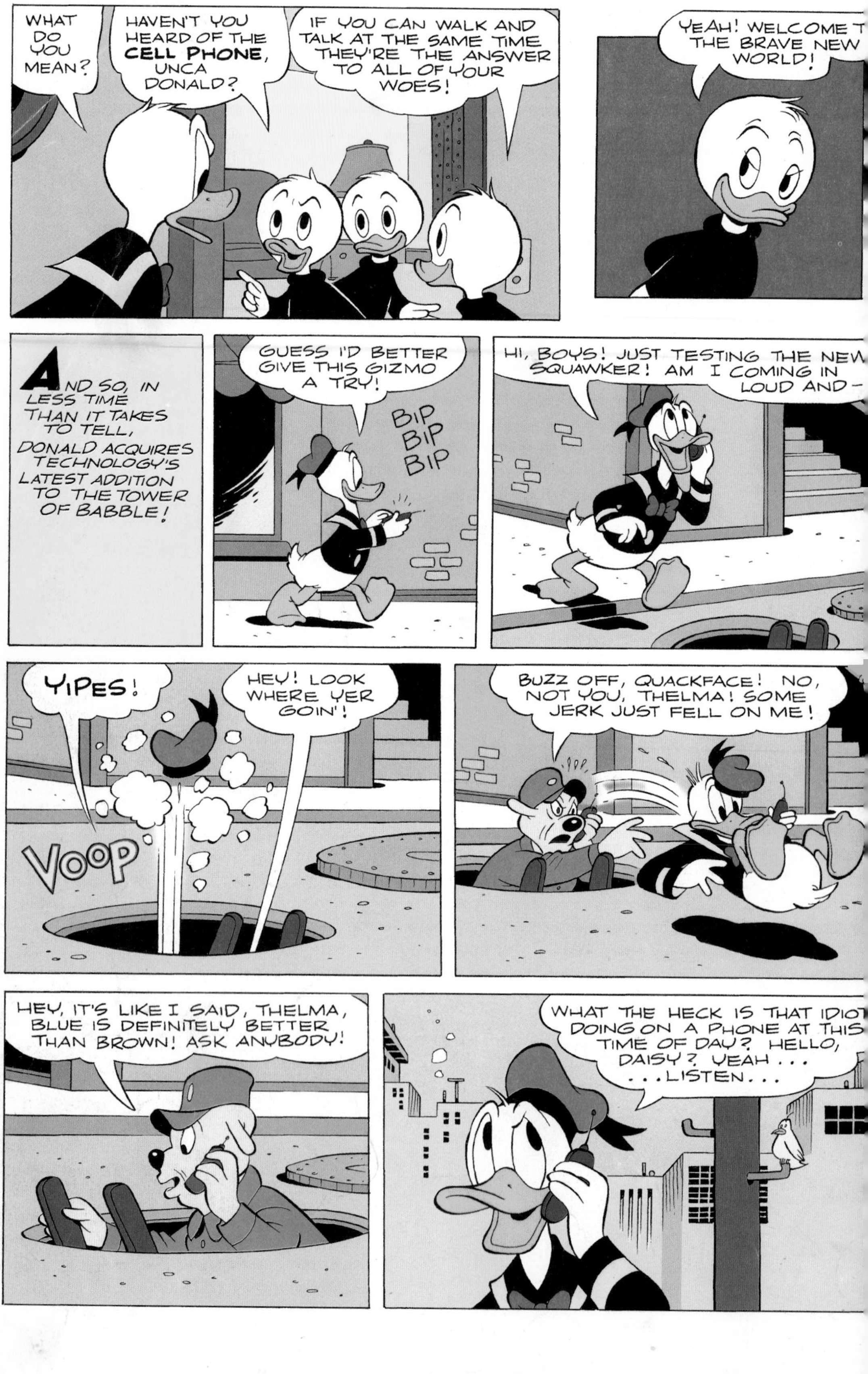
WHAT DO YOU MEAN?
HAVEN'T YOU HEARD OF THE CELL PHONE, UNCA DONALD?
IF YOU CAN WALK AND TALK AT THE SAME TIME THEY'RE THE ANSWER TO ALL OF YOUR WOES!
YEAH! WELCOME T THE BRAVE NEW WORLD!
AND SO, IN LESS TIME THAN IT TAKES TO TELL, DONALD ACQUIRES TECHNOLOGY'S LATEST ADDITION TO THE TOWER OF BABBLE!
GUESS I'D BETTER GIVE THIS GIZMO A TRY!
BIP BIP BIP
HI, BOYS! JUST TESTING THE NEW SQUAWKER! AM I COMING IN LOUD AND—
YIPES!
VOOP
HEY! LOOK WHERE YER GOIN'!
BUZZ OFF, QUACKFACE! NO, NOT YOU, THELMA! SOME JERK JUST FELL ON ME!
HEY, IT'S LIKE I SAID, THELMA, BLUE IS DEFINITELY BETTER THAN BROWN! ASK ANYBODY!
WHAT THE HECK IS THAT IDIOT DOING ON A PHONE AT THIS TIME OF DAY? HELLO, DAISY? YEAH . . . . . . LISTEN . . .

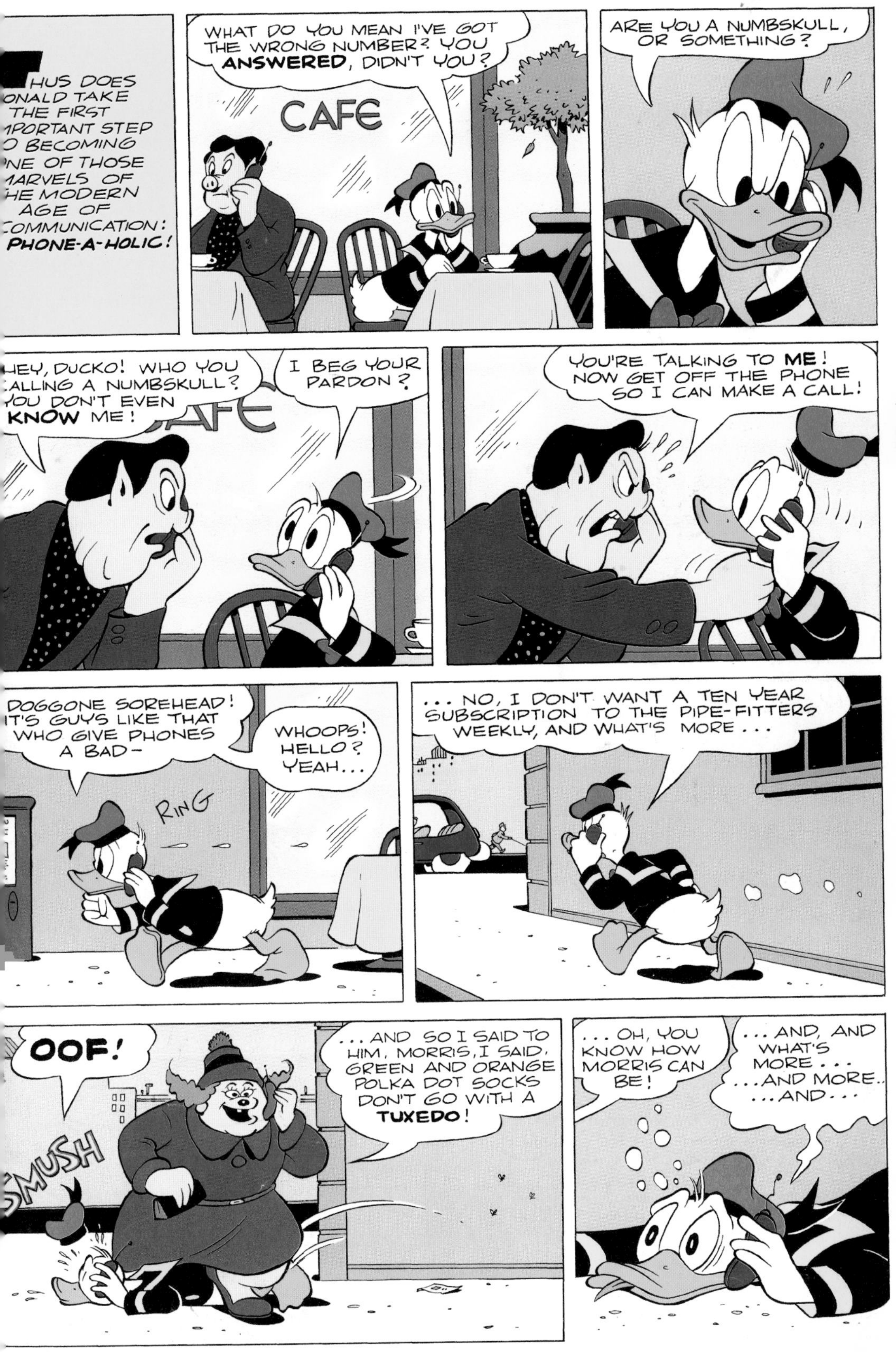

HUS DOES
ONALD TAKE
THE FIRST
MPORTANT STEP
O BECOMING
NE OF THOSE
ARVELS OF
HE MODERN
AGE OF
COMMUNICATION:
PHONE-A-HOLIC!
WHAT DO YOU MEAN I'VE GOT THE WRONG NUMBER? YOU **ANSWERED**, DIDN'T YOU?
CAFE
ARE YOU A NUMBSKULL, OR SOMETHING?
HEY, DUCKO! WHO YOU CALLING A NUMBSKULL? YOU DON'T EVEN **KNOW** ME!
I BEG YOUR PARDON?
YOU'RE TALKING TO **ME**! NOW GET OFF THE PHONE SO I CAN MAKE A CALL!
DOGGONE SOREHEAD! IT'S GUYS LIKE THAT WHO GIVE PHONES A BAD–
WHOOPS! HELLO? YEAH...
RING
... NO, I DON'T WANT A TEN YEAR SUBSCRIPTION TO THE PIPE-FITTERS WEEKLY, AND WHAT'S MORE ...
OOF!
SMUSH
... AND SO I SAID TO HIM, MORRIS, I SAID, GREEN AND ORANGE POLKA DOT SOCKS DON'T GO WITH A **TUXEDO**!
... OH, YOU KNOW HOW MORRIS CAN BE!
... AND, AND WHAT'S MORE ... ... AND MORE.. ... AND ...

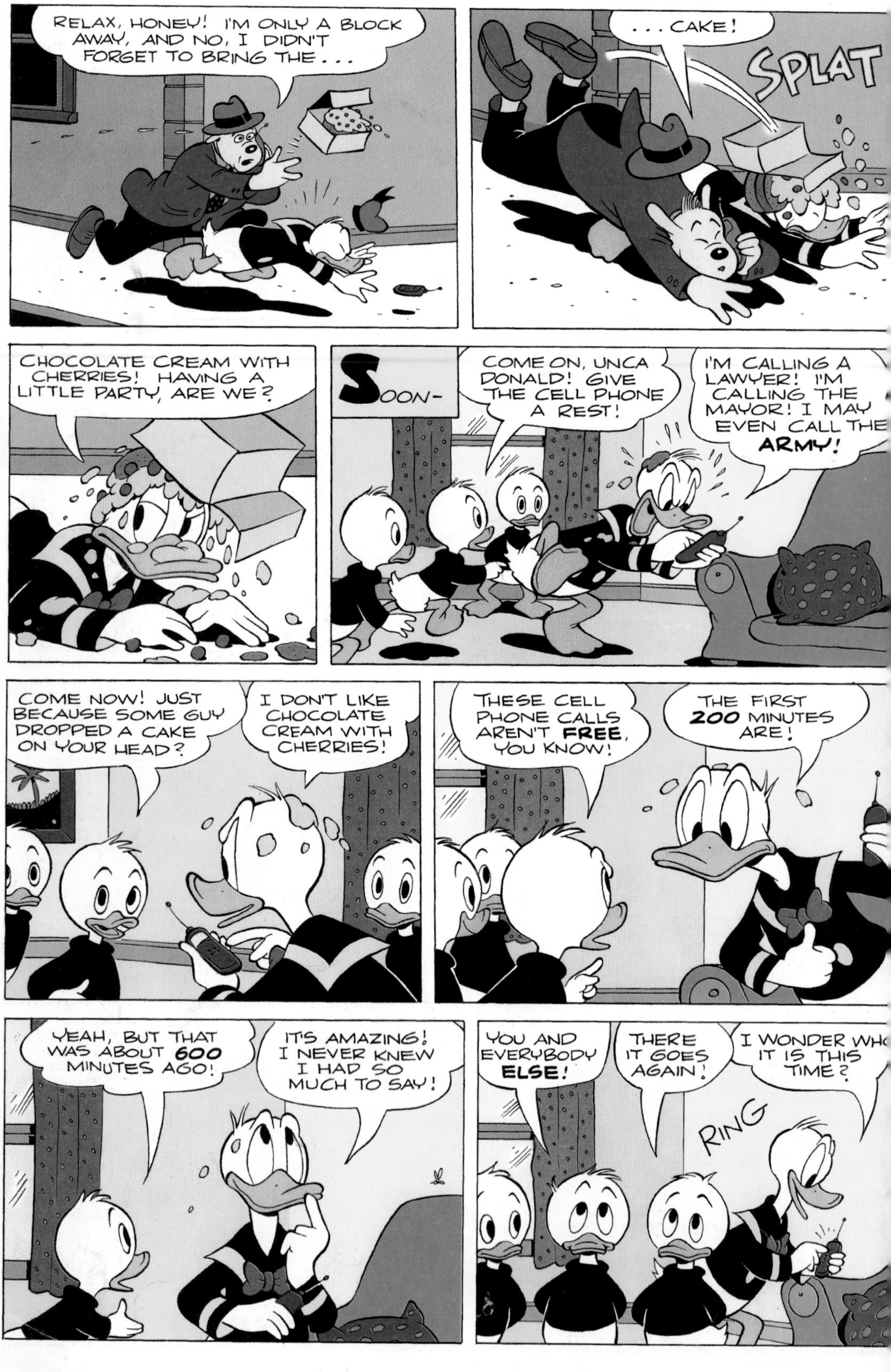
RELAX, HONEY! I'M ONLY A BLOCK AWAY, AND NO, I DIDN'T FORGET TO BRING THE . . .
. . . CAKE!
SPLAT
CHOCOLATE CREAM WITH CHERRIES! HAVING A LITTLE PARTY, ARE WE?
SOON-
COME ON, UNCA DONALD! GIVE THE CELL PHONE A REST!
I'M CALLING A LAWYER! I'M CALLING THE MAYOR! I MAY EVEN CALL THE ARMY!
COME NOW! JUST BECAUSE SOME GUY DROPPED A CAKE ON YOUR HEAD?
I DON'T LIKE CHOCOLATE CREAM WITH CHERRIES!
THESE CELL PHONE CALLS AREN'T FREE, YOU KNOW!
THE FIRST 200 MINUTES ARE!
YEAH, BUT THAT WAS ABOUT 600 MINUTES AGO!
IT'S AMAZING! I NEVER KNEW I HAD SO MUCH TO SAY!
YOU AND EVERYBODY ELSE!
THERE IT GOES AGAIN!
RING
I WONDER WHO IT IS THIS TIME?

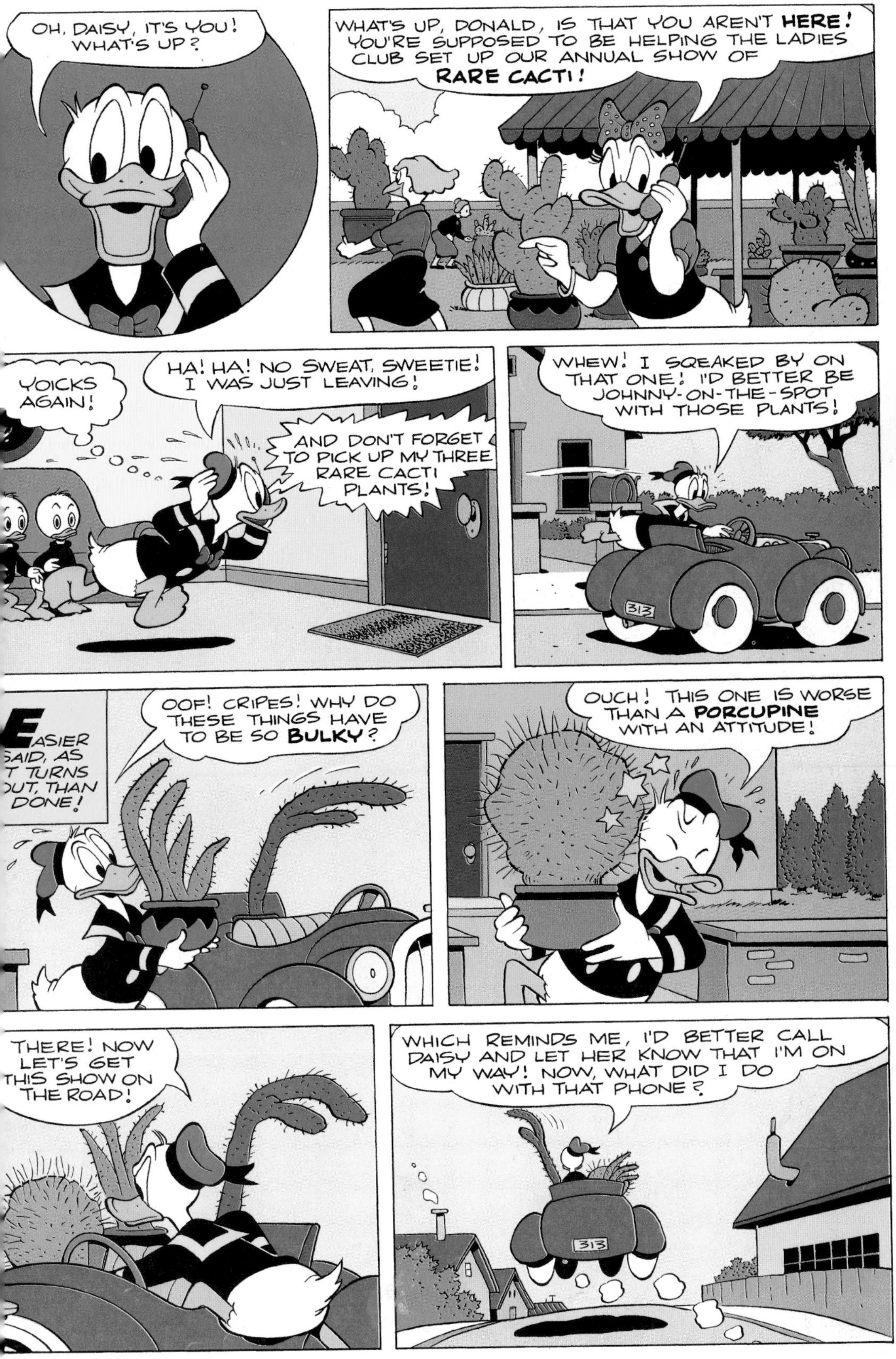
OH, DAISY, IT'S YOU! WHAT'S UP?
WHAT'S UP, DONALD, IS THAT YOU AREN'T **HERE!** YOU'RE SUPPOSED TO BE HELPING THE LADIES CLUB SET UP OUR ANNUAL SHOW OF **RARE CACTI!**
YOICKS AGAIN!
HA! HA! NO SWEAT, SWEETIE! I WAS JUST LEAVING!
AND DON'T FORGET TO PICK UP MY THREE RARE CACTI PLANTS!
WHEW! I SQEAKED BY ON THAT ONE! I'D BETTER BE JOHNNY-ON-THE-SPOT WITH THOSE PLANTS!
313
EASIER SAID, AS IT TURNS OUT, THAN DONE!
OOF! CRIPES! WHY DO THESE THINGS HAVE TO BE SO **BULKY**?
OUCH! THIS ONE IS WORSE THAN A **PORCUPINE** WITH AN ATTITUDE!
THERE! NOW LET'S GET THIS SHOW ON THE ROAD!
WHICH REMINDS ME, I'D BETTER CALL DAISY AND LET HER KNOW THAT I'M ON MY WAY! NOW, WHAT DID I DO WITH THAT PHONE?
313

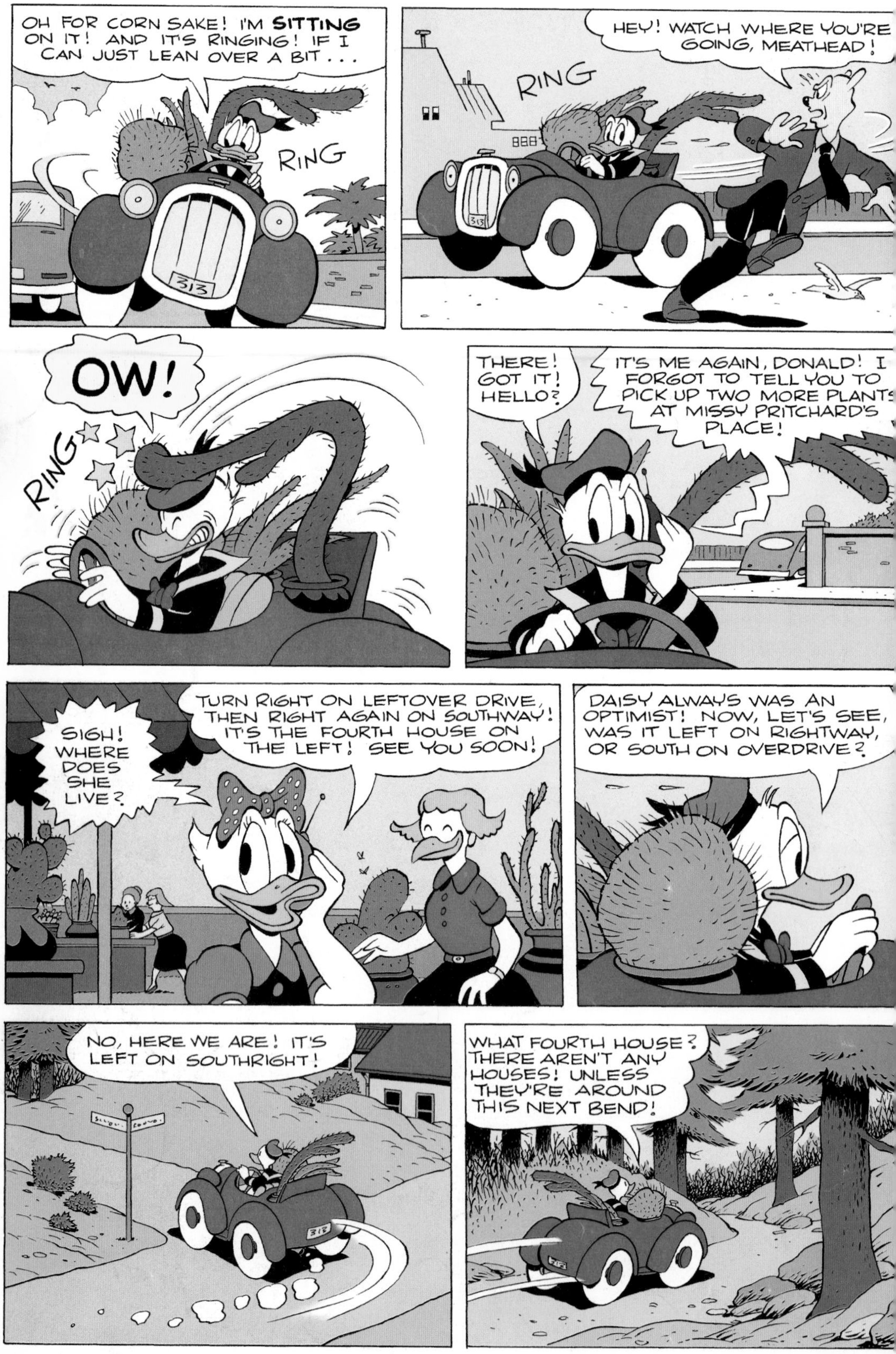
OH FOR CORN SAKE! I'M SITTING ON IT! AND IT'S RINGING! IF I CAN JUST LEAN OVER A BIT . . .
RING
313
HEY! WATCH WHERE YOU'RE GOING, MEATHEAD!
RING
313
OW!
RING
THERE! GOT IT! HELLO?
IT'S ME AGAIN, DONALD! I FORGOT TO TELL YOU TO PICK UP TWO MORE PLANTS AT MISSY PRITCHARD'S PLACE!
SIGH! WHERE DOES SHE LIVE?
TURN RIGHT ON LEFTOVER DRIVE, THEN RIGHT AGAIN ON SOUTHWAY! IT'S THE FOURTH HOUSE ON THE LEFT! SEE YOU SOON!
DAISY ALWAYS WAS AN OPTIMIST! NOW, LET'S SEE, WAS IT LEFT ON RIGHTWAY, OR SOUTH ON OVERDRIVE?
NO, HERE WE ARE! IT'S LEFT ON SOUTHRIGHT!
WHAT FOURTH HOUSE? THERE AREN'T ANY HOUSES! UNLESS THEY'RE AROUND THIS NEXT BEND!

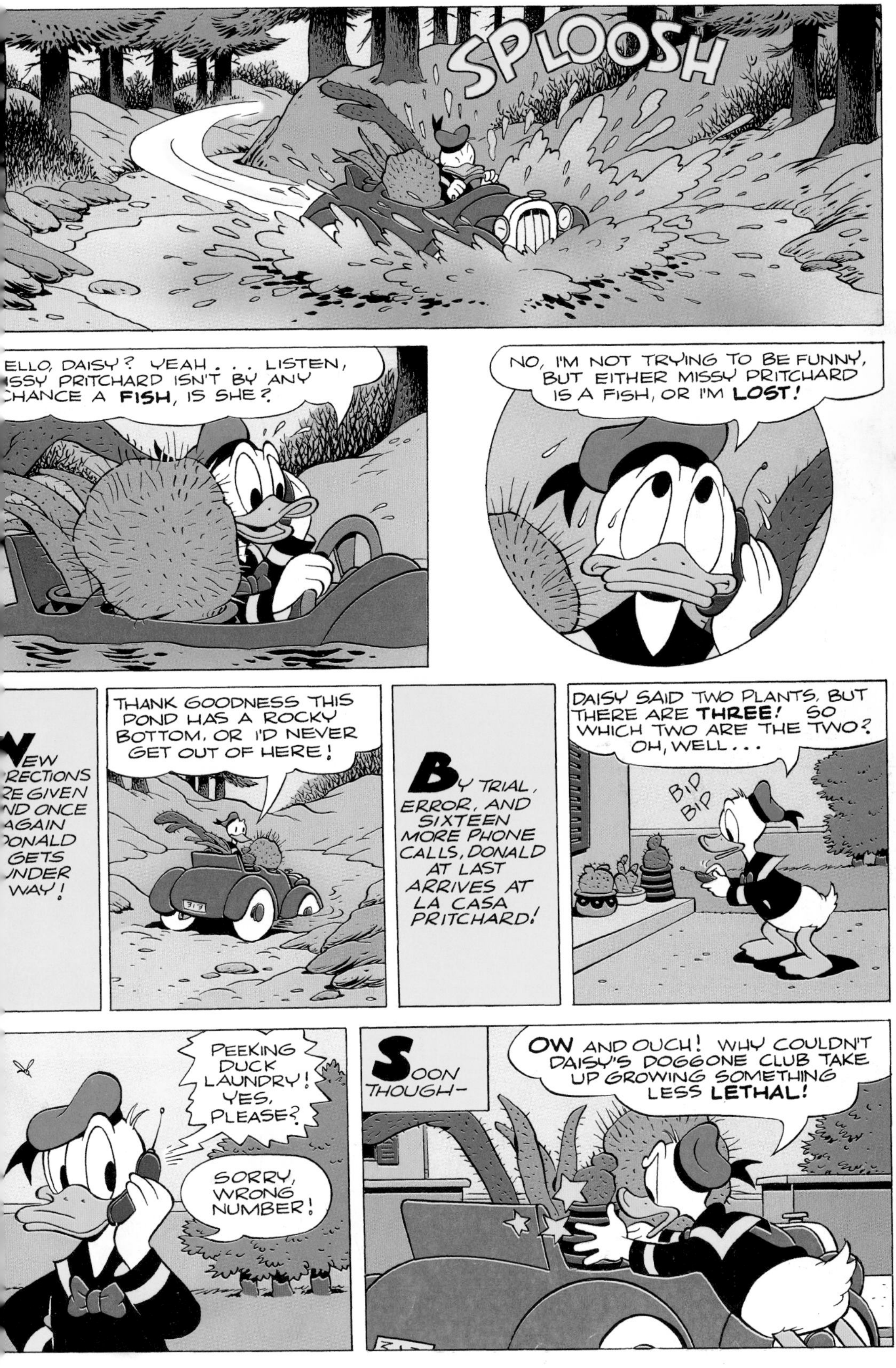
SPLOOSH
ELLO, DAISY? YEAH . . . LISTEN, ISSY PRITCHARD ISN'T BY ANY CHANCE A **FISH**, IS SHE?
NO, I'M NOT TRYING TO BE FUNNY, BUT EITHER MISSY PRITCHARD IS A FISH, OR I'M **LOST**!
NEW RECTIONS RE GIVEN ND ONCE AGAIN DONALD GETS UNDER WAY!
THANK GOODNESS THIS POND HAS A ROCKY BOTTOM, OR I'D NEVER GET OUT OF HERE!
BY TRIAL, ERROR, AND SIXTEEN MORE PHONE CALLS, DONALD AT LAST ARRIVES AT LA CASA PRITCHARD!
DAISY SAID TWO PLANTS, BUT THERE ARE **THREE**! SO WHICH TWO ARE THE TWO? OH, WELL . . .
BIP BIP
PEEKING DUCK LAUNDRY! YES, PLEASE?
SORRY, WRONG NUMBER!
SOON THOUGH-
OW AND OUCH! WHY COULDN'T DAISY'S DOGGONE CLUB TAKE UP GROWING SOMETHING LESS **LETHAL**!

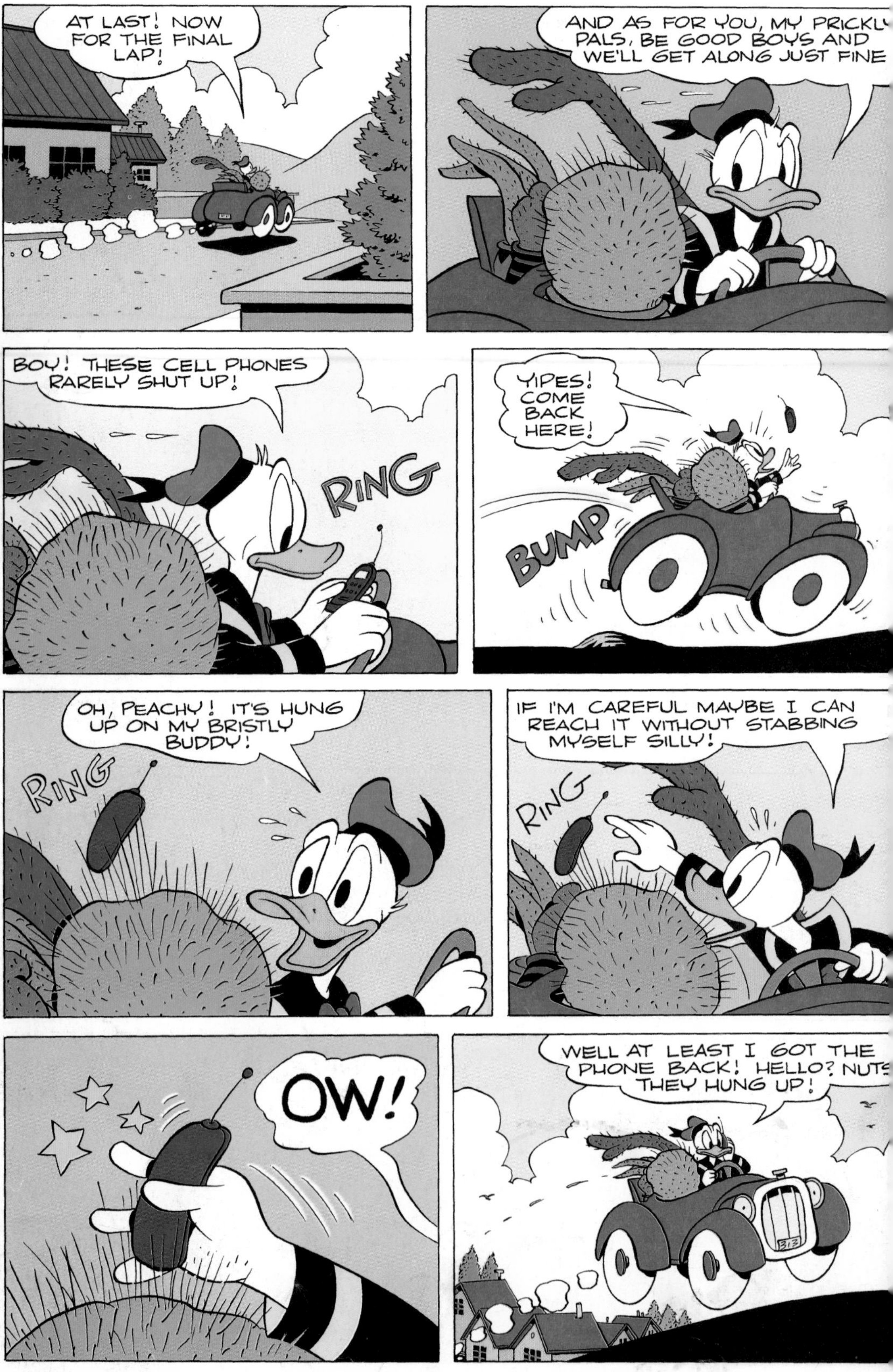
AT LAST! NOW FOR THE FINAL LAP!
AND AS FOR YOU, MY PRICKLY PALS, BE GOOD BOYS AND WE'LL GET ALONG JUST FINE
BOY! THESE CELL PHONES RARELY SHUT UP!
RING
YIPES! COME BACK HERE!
BUMP
OH, PEACHY! IT'S HUNG UP ON MY BRISTLY BUDDY!
RING
IF I'M CAREFUL MAYBE I CAN REACH IT WITHOUT STABBING MYSELF SILLY!
RING
OW!
WELL AT LEAST I GOT THE PHONE BACK! HELLO? NUTS THEY HUNG UP!

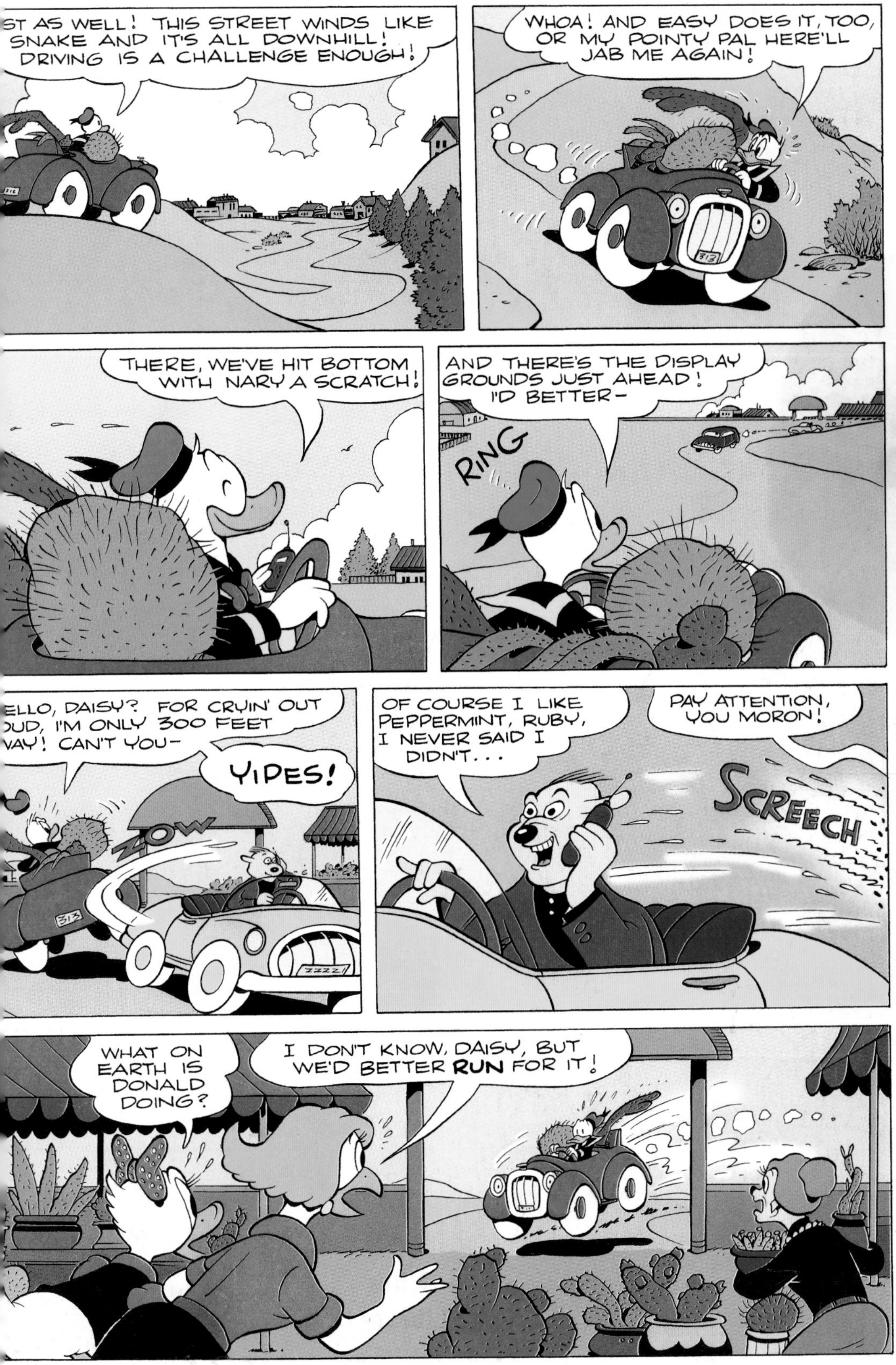

ST AS WELL! THIS STREET WINDS LIKE SNAKE AND IT'S ALL DOWNHILL! DRIVING IS A CHALLENGE ENOUGH!
WHOA! AND EASY DOES IT, TOO, OR MY POINTY PAL HERE'LL JAB ME AGAIN!
THERE, WE'VE HIT BOTTOM WITH NARY A SCRATCH!
AND THERE'S THE DISPLAY GROUNDS JUST AHEAD! I'D BETTER–
RING
ELLO, DAISY? FOR CRYIN' OUT OUD, I'M ONLY 300 FEET WAY! CAN'T YOU–
YIPES!
ZOW
OF COURSE I LIKE PEPPERMINT, RUBY, I NEVER SAID I DIDN'T...
PAY ATTENTION, YOU MORON!
SCREECH
WHAT ON EARTH IS DONALD DOING?
I DON'T KNOW, DAISY, BUT WE'D BETTER RUN FOR IT!

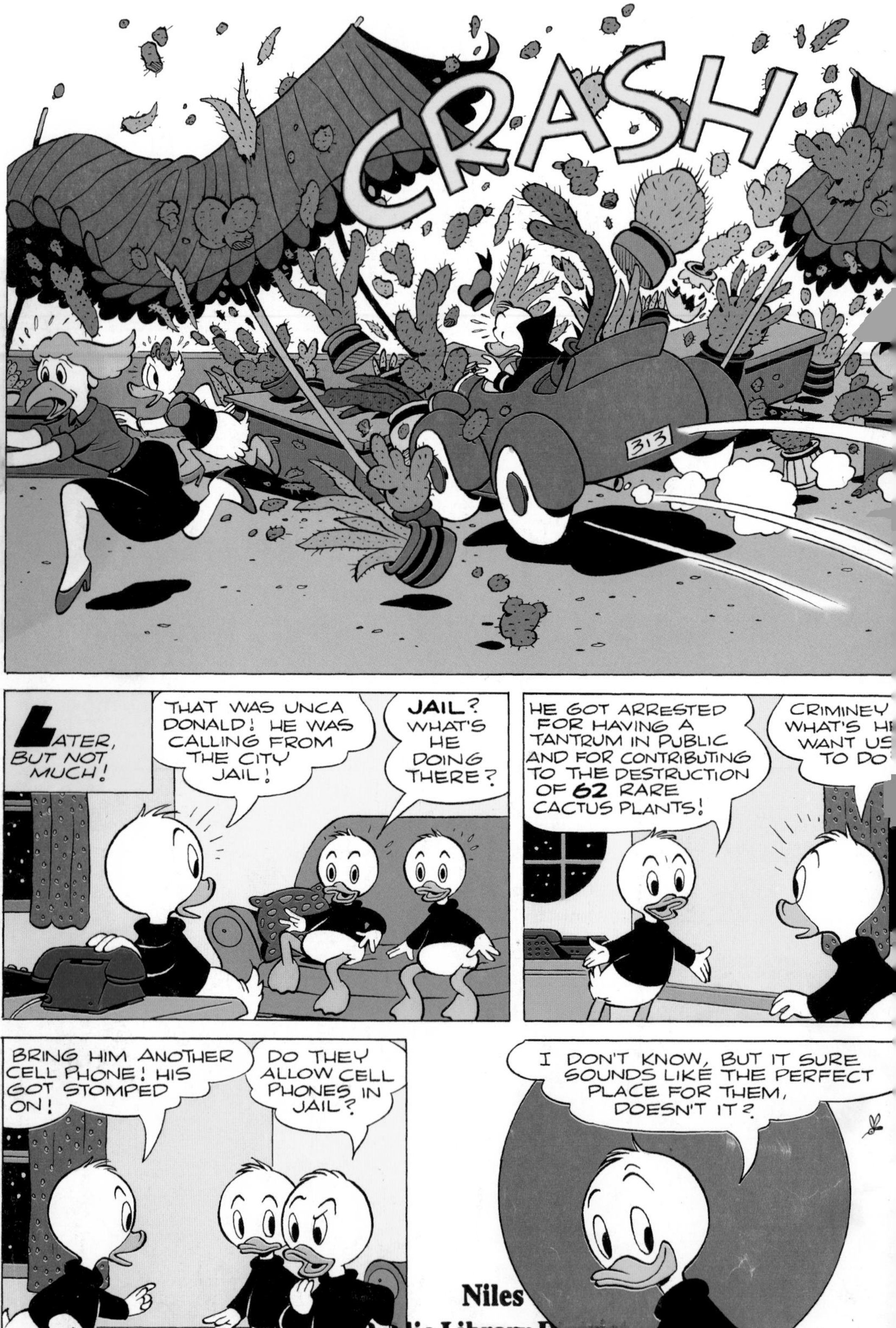
CRASH
LATER, BUT NOT MUCH!
THAT WAS UNCA DONALD! HE WAS CALLING FROM THE CITY JAIL!
JAIL? WHAT'S HE DOING THERE?
HE GOT ARRESTED FOR HAVING A TANTRUM IN PUBLIC AND FOR CONTRIBUTING TO THE DESTRUCTION OF 62 RARE CACTUS PLANTS!
CRIMINEY
BRING HIM ANOTHER CELL PHONE! HIS GOT STOMPED ON!
DO THEY ALLOW CELL PHONES IN JAIL?
I DON'T KNOW, BUT IT SURE SOUNDS LIKE THE PERFECT PLACE FOR THEM, DOESN'T IT?